AMERICA ★ THE ★ BEAUTIFUL

How to Use This Book

Look for these special features in this book:

SIDEBARS, **CHARTS**, **GRAPHS**, and original **MAPS** expand your understanding of what's being discussed—and also make useful sources for classroom reports.

FAQs answer common **F**requently **A**sked **Q**uestions about people, places, and things.

WOW FACTORS offer "Who knew?" facts to keep you thinking.

TRAVEL GUIDE gives you tips on exploring the state—either in person or right from your chair!

PROJECT ROOM provides fun ideas for school assignments and incredible research projects. Plus, there's a guide to primary sources—what they are and how to cite them.

Please note: All statistics are as up-to-date as possible at the time of publication. Population data is taken from the 2010 census.

Consultants: Janet Ellingson, Professor of History, University of Utah; Michael D. Hylland, Utah Geological Survey; William Loren Katz; Brian Cannon, Associate Professor of History, Brigham Young University

Book production by The Design Lab

Library of Congress Cataloging-in-Publication Data
Kent, Deborah.
 Utah / by Deborah Kent. — Revised edition.
   pages cm. — (America the beautiful, third series)
 Includes bibliographical references and index.
 Audience: Ages 9–12.
 ISBN 978-0-531-28295-3 (library binding : alk. paper)
 1. Utah—Juvenile literature. I. Title.
 F826.3.K46 2014
 979.2—dc23   2013046227

1 2 3 4 5 6 7 8 9 10 R 24 23 22 21 20 19 18 17 16 15

America the Beautiful

Utah

BY DEBORAH KENT

Third Series, Revised Edition

Children's Press®
An Imprint of Scholastic Inc.
New York ★ Toronto ★ London ★ Auckland ★ Sydney
Mexico City ★ New Delhi ★ Hong Kong
Danbury, Connecticut

CONTENTS

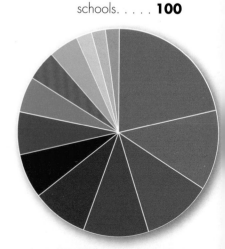

GROWTH AND CHANGE

4

White settlers force Utah's Native Americans onto reservations, and the Mormon community grows, sometimes in conflict with the rest of the nation. **48**

MORE MODERN TIMES

5

Immigrants pour into Utah to work in the mines. Utahns of all backgrounds survive war and the Depression. **62**

9 TRAVEL GUIDE

Utah's national parks, historic sites, and many museums will keep you busy. **106**

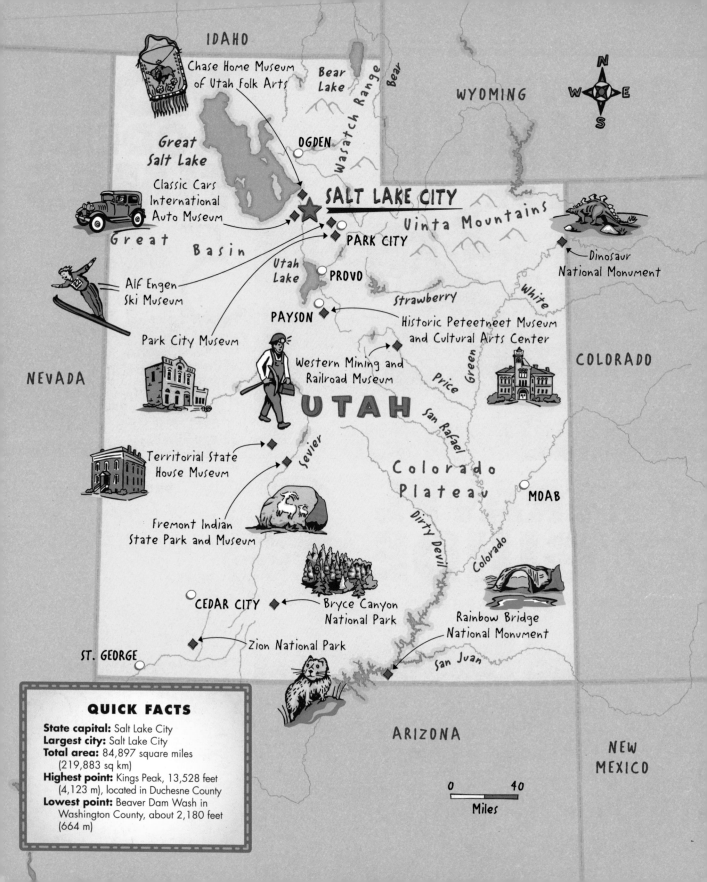

IDAHO

Chase Home Museum
of Utah Folk Arts

Bear
Lake

WYOMING

Great
Salt Lake

OGDEN

Wasatch Range

Bear

Classic Cars
International
Auto Museum

SALT LAKE CITY

Uinta Mountains

Dinosaur
National Monument

Great   Basin

PARK CITY

Utah
Lake

PROVO

Strawberry

White

Alf Engen
Ski Museum

PAYSON

Historic Peteetneet Museum
and Cultural Arts Center

Park City Museum

Western Mining and
Railroad Museum

UTAH

Price

Green

San Rafael

COLORADO

NEVADA

Territorial State
House Museum

Sevier

Colorado
Plateau

MOAB

Fremont Indian
State Park and Museum

Dirty Devil

Colorado

Bryce Canyon
National Park

Rainbow Bridge
National Monument

CEDAR CITY

Zion National Park

San Juan

ST. GEORGE

ARIZONA

NEW
MEXICO

0   40
Miles

Welcome to Utah!

HOW DID UTAH GET ITS NAME?

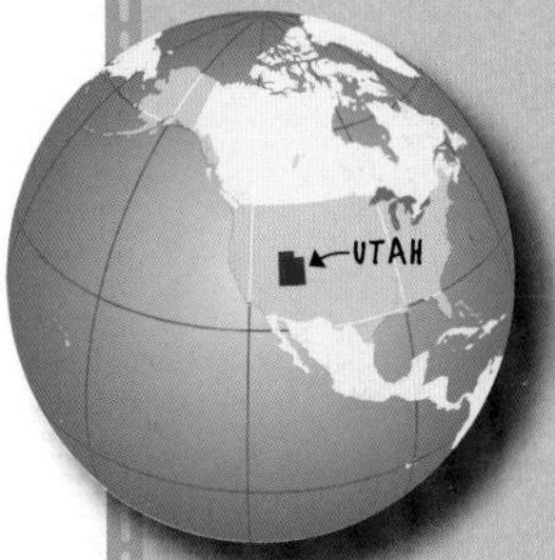

In 1850, white settlers in present-day Utah asked Congress to make their land a U.S. territory. Congress agreed and named the territory Utah. No one is entirely sure where the name "Utah" came from. One of the most common theories is that it came from an Apache word meaning "upper" or "higher up." This term also refers to another Native American group, known today as Utes.

←UTAH

COLORADO

KANSAS

OKLAHOMA

NEW
MEXICO

TEXAS

READ ABOUT

The Thor's Hammer
rock formation
in Bryce Canyon
National Park

CHAPTER ONE

LAND

★

DAZZLING, BREATHTAKING, AND STUNNING. When people try to describe Utah's 84,897 square miles (219,883 square kilometers) of land, the English language seems to run out of words. Utah is a state of towering summits. Kings Peak, its highest point, stands at 13,528 feet (4,123 meters), and even its lowest point rises 2,180 feet (664 m) above sea level at Beaver Dam Wash. Throughout the state, wind and water have carved rock formations into fantastic shapes. Even Utah's deserts have a haunting beauty. Utah is a land that you must see to believe.

FOUR STATES HERE MEET IN FREE...

Utah Geo-Facts

Along with the state's geographical highlights, this chart ranks Utah's land, water, and total area compared to all other states.

Total area; rank	84,897 square miles (219,883 sq km); 13th
Land; rank	82,191 square miles (212,875 sq km); 12th
Water; rank	2,706 square miles (7,009 sq km); 17th
Inland water; rank	2,706 square miles (7,009 sq km); 8th
Geographic center	Sanpete Valley, 3 miles (5 km) north of Manti
Latitude	37° N to 42° N
Longitude	109° W to 114° W
Highest point	Kings Peak, 13,528 feet (4,123 m), located in Duchesne County
Lowest point	Beaver Dam Wash in Washington County, about 2,180 feet (664 m)
Largest city	Salt Lake City
Longest rivers	Colorado and Green

Source: U.S. Census Bureau

The states of Arizona, New Mexico, and Colorado all meet at Utah's southeastern corner. This "Four Corners" area is the only place in the country where four states meet.

At this spot on the Navajo Indian Reservation, the states of Colorado, Utah, Arizona, and New Mexico meet.

GETTING TO KNOW UTAH

Utah lies in the western United States. Its boundaries are razor straight, ignoring rivers and other natural divisions. On a map, Utah looks like a large rectangle with a piece cut out of the northeastern corner. Idaho lies to the north, and Wyoming nestles into the

Utah Topography

Use the color-coded elevation chart to see on the map Utah's high points (dark red to orange) and low points (green). Elevation is measured as the distance above or below sea level.

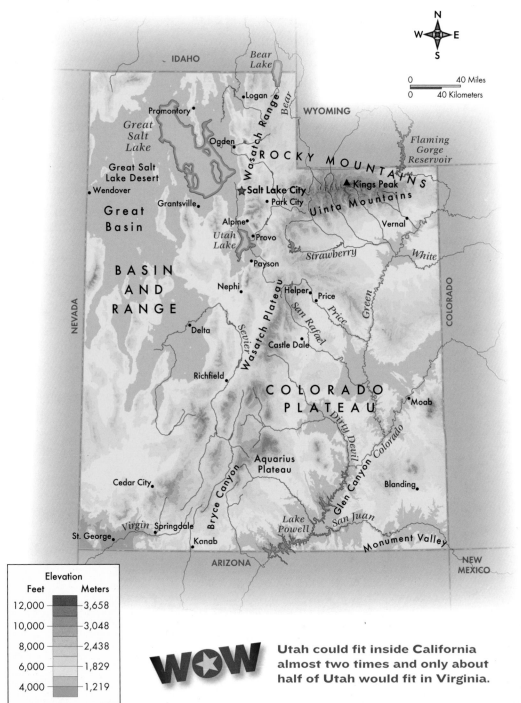

Elevation	
Feet	Meters
12,000	3,658
10,000	3,048
8,000	2,438
6,000	1,829
4,000	1,219

WOW Utah could fit inside California almost two times and only about half of Utah would fit in Virginia.

cutout northeastern section. To the east is Colorado. Arizona is south of Utah, and Nevada lies to the west.

SHAPING THE LAND

Over hundreds of millions of years, many forces shaped the land that is Utah today. Mountains have risen up where **tectonic plates** in the earth's outer layer pushed against each other and pulled apart. Other mountains emerged when lava erupted through cracks in the earth's surface, forcing the ground upward.

Geological forces have also given Utah a wealth of natural resources, including copper, gold, silver, and **molybdenum** from Bingham Canyon; salt from Great Salt Lake; and coal, oil, and natural gas.

Gulls and other birds on the Great Salt Lake, as seen from the Antelope Island Causeway

Utah straddles the boundary between the Rocky Mountains and what geologists call the Basin and Range Province. Much of western Utah falls within the Basin and Range. At the eastern edge of the basin floor, the Rockies rise dramatically. The Colorado Plateau takes up most of Utah's lower right triangle.

Basin and Range Province

The Basin and Range Province sweeps from southeastern Oregon all the way to Texas. This region is made up of ranges of mountains running north to south. Between these ranges lie flat-bottomed valleys, or basins.

An outstanding feature of the Basin and Range Province in Utah is Great Salt Lake, the last remnant of Lake Bonneville, a vast lake that thousands of years ago covered about one-fourth of today's Utah. Several rivers flow into Great Salt Lake, including the Bear, Jordan, and Weber. Because its water is so salty, Great Salt Lake is sometimes referred to as an inland sea.

Another amazing remnant of Lake Bonneville is the Bonneville Salt Flats. From the earliest days of the automobile, the salt flat in northwestern Utah has proved irresistible to drivers who want to find out how fast they can go. This stretch of land is flat as a tabletop and unbroken by roads.

For thousands of years, the gentle action of Lake Bonneville's currents and deposits of silt and clay smoothed its floor. As the lake evaporated, salt remained on the flat bottom. Water very near the surface holds the salt crystals together, so only tiny amounts of salt blow away in the wind. Also, when it rains, the rainwater dissolves salt at the surface and then carries it to the low-lying places to which the water flows. The salt dries up when the rainwater evaporates. In this way, low-lying areas get filled in, and over time the ground surface becomes very flat.

If you boil 1 quart (1 liter) of water from the saltiest part of Great Salt Lake, you will be left with about a half a cup (0.12 liters) of salt!

Q8 WHY IS GREAT SALT LAKE SO SALTY?

A8 As Lake Bonneville dried up, salt and other minerals were left behind. Because the shrinking lake had no stream out to the sea, the salt deposits became concentrated in the lake.

Quaking aspen trees on Superior Peak in the Wasatch Mountains

WORD TO KNOW

tributary *a river that flows into a larger river*

The Colorado Plateau in Utah is as rich in dinosaur fossils as any area in the world.

Colorado Plateau

From the point where the Four Corners meet, the Colorado Plateau reaches out into Utah, Colorado, Arizona, and New Mexico. If you picture a diagonal line from Utah's southwestern corner to the northeast, most of the state below that line is in the Colorado Plateau region. This is Utah's biggest land region, covering nearly half of its area.

The Colorado River and its main **tributary**, the Green River, course through this region. Rivers and streams erode deep canyons and gorges into layers of rock, uncovering evidence of dinosaurs.

Throughout the Colorado Plateau, rocks form natural pillars and arches layered in pink, red, and green. Here and there, great flat rocks called fins stand on edge, like plates balanced on their rims.

Rocky Mountain Region

The Rockies are a series of mountain ranges that stretch from Canada to Mexico. Two ranges of the Rockies, the Wasatch Range and the Uinta Mountains, cross northern Utah. The western edge of the Wasatch Range rises steeply from the basin floor. Farther east, the mountains are less dramatic, and the range is broken with fertile valleys.

Near Coalville, the Uintas veer eastward from the Wasatch Range into Colorado. The Uintas are among the few mountain ranges in North America that run east to west instead of north to south. Utah's highest peaks, including Kings Peak, stand in this range.

CLIMATE

Utah is the second-driest state in the country. Only Nevada gets less rain over the course of a year. On average, Utah has about 250 sunny days each year. Parts of the Basin and Range Province and the Colorado Plateau may receive just a few inches of rain annually.

When rainstorms hit Utah's desert regions, they tend to hit hard. A sudden downpour might turn a parched desert streambed into a raging torrent. Such flash floods can sweep away any animals or humans in their path.

Utah's desert regions endure broiling hot summers, but the winters tend to be mild. In the desert town of Moab, the average high temperature in July is 99 degrees Fahrenheit (37 degrees Celsius).

Weather Report

TEMPERATURE 117°F

TEMPERATURE -50°F

This chart shows record temperatures (high and low) for the state, as well as average temperatures (July and January) and average annual precipitation.

Record high temperature . . . . 117°F (47°C) at St. George on July 5, 1985

Record low temperature . . . . –50°F (–46°C) at East Portal on January 5, 1913

Average July temperature, Salt Lake City . . . . 79°F (26°C)

Average January temperature, Salt Lake City . . . . 30°F (–1°C)

Average yearly precipitation, Salt Lake City . . 16 inches (41 cm)

Source: National Climatic Data Center, NESDIS, NOAA, U.S. Dept. of Commerce

Skiers at the Snowbird Ski and Summer Resort

Bristlecone pines are the oldest trees in the world. Some bristlecones in Utah are 3,000 years old!

If you want to escape the summer heat, just climb a mountain. In Park City, the average temperature in July is only about 65°F (18°C). Some of Utah's tallest peaks wear crowns of snow through most of the year. Mountain roads can close as early as October and as late as May when masses of heavy snow break loose and tumble down a mountainside in an avalanche. Between 1847 and 1949, 189 people died in Utah avalanches. From 1950 to 2013, avalanches killed more than 100 people in Utah.

PLANT LIFE

By looking at the trees and plants, you can get a good idea of which region of Utah you are in. In much of the Rocky Mountain Region, the soil is rich and moist. The mountains are green with aspen, fir, spruce, and pine trees. Much of the Basin and Range Province is covered with sagebrush and a tough, hardy grass called cheatgrass. Some cotton-woods and willows grow along the streams. Small trees such as piñon pine and juniper grow in the mountains.

The plants and trees of the Colorado Plateau have also adapted to rugged conditions. On the lower mountainsides, creosote and mesquite bushes grow. Some sagebrush and cheatgrass can also be found. The mountains are speckled with trees such as scrub oak, juniper, mountain ash, yellow pine, bristlecone pine, and Douglas fir. Cactus grows in both the Colorado Plateau and the Basin and Range Province.

For a few brief weeks in spring, Utah's deserts burst into bloom. Flowering sagebrush fills the air with fragrance. Red blooms on the claret cup cactus and pink and yellow on the beavertail cactus bring bright colors to a subdued landscape. The sego lily, Utah's state flower, blossoms throughout the state. The mountains and high plateaus are blanketed with dogtooth violets, sweet William, and other wildflowers. The orange and red spikes of the Indian paintbrush brighten dry canyons.

ENDANGERED PLANTS

A number of plant species in Utah are listed as threatened or endangered with extinction. Endangered wildflowers include the dwarf bearclaw poppy, Welsh's milkweed, Deseret milkvetch, and Maguire primrose. Several desert cactus species are also endangered, including the Uinta Basin hookless cactus, Winkler pincushion cactus, and San Rafael cactus.

Blooms of the claret cup cactus

SEE IT HERE!

ANTELOPE ISLAND STATE PARK

Antelope Island is the largest of Great Salt Lake's ten islands. Antelope Island State Park is located here, home to a herd of 550 to 700 wild bison. The bison were brought to the island in 1893 in an effort to protect the animals when they were on the verge of extinction. Other wildlife on the island includes mule deer, pronghorn, and desert bighorn sheep. In spring and fall, thousands of migrating birds pause on the island to feast on the tiny brine shrimp that live in the lake.

A moose grazes in an Albion Basin meadow.

ANIMAL LIFE

Utah's deserts and canyons may seem lifeless to the casual observer, but they shelter a host of animals. Snakes, lizards, and tortoises sun themselves on rocks or burrow into the ground when the day grows hot. Forested areas shelter coyotes, bobcats, raccoons, skunks, and weasels. Muskrats and beavers build their houses along the streams. The last grizzlies disappeared from Utah's forests in the 1920s, but the state is still home to many black bears. In some areas, the once-scarce cougar, or mountain lion, is making a comeback.

Mule deer graze in Utah's valleys and on its grassy mountainsides. Other grazing animals include moose, elk, desert bighorn sheep, mountain goats, and pronghorn. Some wild horses, known as mustangs, live in western Utah. The state also has small herds of bison in the Henry Mountains and at Antelope Island State Park.

A wide variety of game fish thrive in Utah's streams and freshwater lakes. Several species of trout can be found, as can bass, perch, and whitefish.

ENDANGERED ANIMALS

Utah has a number of animal species that are listed as threatened or endangered. Among the state's endangered fish are the humpback chub, the razorback sucker, and the Colorado pikeminnow. Among the state's endangered birds are the whooping crane and the southwestern willow flycatcher. Mammals on the endangered list are the black-footed ferret, the Canada lynx, and the Utah prairie dog. The desert tortoise is a reptile that is considered threatened.

The Utah prairie dog is one of the animals on the state's endangered list.

CARING FOR THE LAND

Some of Utah's unique natural features are protected as national parks and national monuments. Millions of visitors flock to the Beehive State each year to gaze spellbound at the state's wonders.

Though Utahns cherish their state's natural beauty, humans have often had a harmful impact on the environment. Water is a scarce resource in Utah, and great demands are placed on the state's limited supply. Dams and other projects bring water to thirsty farmland but deplete rivers and streams. Chemical fertilizers and pesticides have polluted precious waterways. The plants and animals of Utah's fragile desert environment are vanishing as the human population grows.

In the first years of the 21st century, oil and logging companies pushed for the right to operate in Utah's

FAQ

Q8 WHY IS UTAH CALLED THE BEEHIVE STATE?

A8 Most of Utah's early white settlers belonged to the Church of Jesus Christ of Latter-day Saints, which follows a holy book called the Book of Mormon. They were hard workers, and they saw their territory as a hive of industry. They wanted to call their new state Deseret, which means "honeybee" in the Book of Mormon.

MINI-BIO

TERRY TEMPEST WILLIAMS: A VOICE FOR WILD PLACES

As a child growing up in Salt Lake City, Terry Tempest Williams (1955–) loved family trips to the Bear River Migratory Bird Refuge. Williams became concerned about damage to the environment caused by human activities. She has written many books about Utah's mountains and deserts, calling for the protection of the state's wild places. Her books include *Refuge: An Unnatural History of Family and Place*, which discusses damage done to the Bear River refuge.

? **Want to know more?** Visit www.factsfornow .scholastic.com and enter the keyword **Utah**.

remote areas. In 2002, the federal government opened the area near Arches and Canyonlands National Parks to oil exploration and drilling. Meanwhile, environmentalists fought to save the state's untouched forests, deserts, and canyons. In 2007, the federal Bureau of Land Management (BLM) delayed allowing drilling on a portion of Utah land to protect the habitat of a threatened bird called the sage grouse. Today, the BLM has leased 4.3 million acres (1.7 million hectares) in Utah for oil and gas drilling and has withdrawn another 5 million acres (2 million ha) from drilling to protect archaeological and natural sites. Utah environmentalists continue to fight to ensure a healthy future for their state.

THINK ABOUT IT!

Living with Less

Most Utahns value the environment, but they also want to live in comfort, with the conveniences of modern life. Some environmentalists argue that humans must learn to make fewer demands on the land. Historian and environmental writer Donald Worster states, "The primary thing that is necessary today, especially for people living in areas such as Utah where vital natural resources are scarce, is to get control of one's needs. That is, to determine which are our real needs and which are the needs that we've just invented, created, or thought up."

Utah National Park Areas

This map shows some of Utah's national parks, monuments, preserves, and other areas protected by the National Park Service.

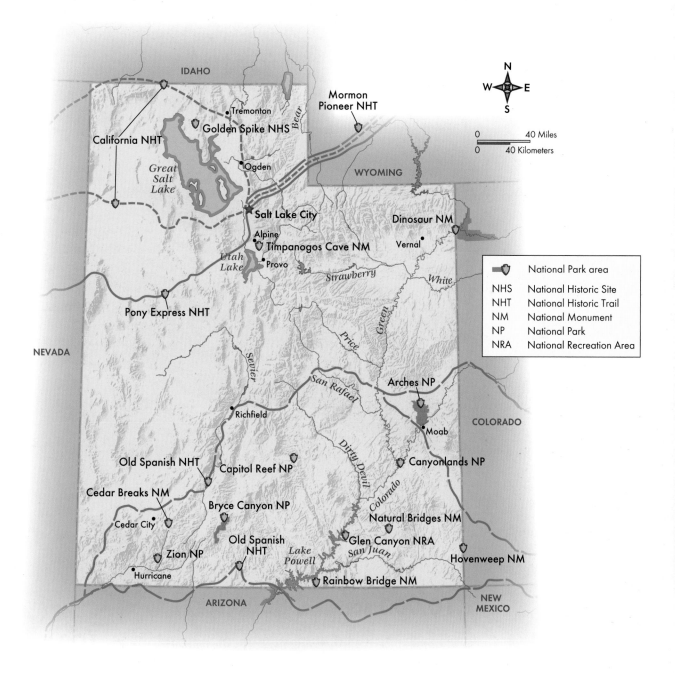

READ ABOUT

Remains of Ancestral Pueblo cliff dwellings in Cedar Mesa

c.10,000 BCE

The first humans reach present-day Utah

c. 8000 BCE

Desert Archaic people begin to live in the marshes around Lake Bonneville

▲ **c. 100 CE**

Ancestral Pueblo people appear in the Four Corners region

CHAPTER TWO

FIRST PEOPLE

★

IN 2004, SCHOLARS BEGAN TO EXPLORE A SITE IN UTAH'S BOOK CLIFFS AREA. They found arrowheads and clay beads scattered on the ground and untouched paintings adorning stone cliffs. They discovered hundreds of ancient dwellings and the mummified bodies of people who lived 4,000 years ago. The site at Book Cliffs is one of many places where scientists are gathering information about Utah's first people.

c. 1250
Ancestral Pueblo people suddenly abandon their villages and move south

c. 1300
Shoshoneans move into Utah

1600s ▶
Horses are introduced to Native people in the region

These petroglyphs were created by ancient peoples and appear in Canyonlands National Park.

People lived in Danger Cave near Wendover for some 7,000 years, beginning around 9000 BCE. Because the cave is very dry, fabrics, nets, bone tools, and even leftovers from dinner were preserved from decay.

THE PALEO-INDIANS

Human beings probably reached the land now called Utah sometime around 10,000 BCE. They were the descendants of people who entered North America about 20,000 years ago. Ocean levels were much lower then, exposing a land bridge between North America and Asia. People walked over the bridge from Asia to what is now Alaska. From there they spread throughout North America.

Utah's earliest people, called Paleo-Indians, lived in small, scattered bands in the marshes along the shores of Lake Bonneville. They fished, hunted, and gathered wild roots and berries. They hunted with spears, their points chipped carefully from stone.

THE DESERT ARCHAIC PEOPLE

Sometime around 8000 BCE, a new group of people arrived in Utah. Like the Paleo-Indians, the Desert Archaic people lived in the marshes around the lake. Cattails and other marsh plants provided much of their food. But they hunted differently from the Paleo-Indians. They used an atlatl, a tool designed for launching spears. Atlatls allowed the Desert Archaic people to hunt rabbits, deer, and other game with better accuracy.

As time progressed, Lake Bonneville grew smaller and smaller. The marshes disappeared, and the Desert Archaic people searched for food in the mountains and canyons. By about 2,000 years ago, the people were gone. Some scientists believe that they moved eastward into the Four Corners region. The Desert Archaic people may be the ancestors of the group known as the Ancestral Pueblo people.

MINI-BIO

JESSE D. JENNINGS: FATHER OF UTAH ARCHAEOLOGY

After graduating from college in his native New Mexico, Jesse D. Jennings (1909–1997) joined the Department of Anthropology—the study of human cultures—at the University of Chicago. Every anthropology student had to spend time working on an **archaeological** dig. Digging and dirt came naturally to Jennings, who had grown up on a farm. He was hooked! He led expeditions to explore Danger Cave and other ancient sites. He taught at the University of Utah and founded the Utah Museum of Natural History.

? **Want to know more?** Visit www.factsfornow .scholastic.com and enter the keyword **Utah**.

WORD TO KNOW

archaeological *related to the study of the remains of past human societies*

ANCIENT ART

A maze of steep-walled canyons threads the high country of southeastern Utah. Ancient people adorned the walls of hundreds of these canyons with paintings. Archaeologists are trying to confirm the dates, but the paintings may have been made as long as 7,000 years ago. The most spectacular of these rock paintings is a giant mural at Horseshoe Canyon near Price. The painting stretches nearly 300 feet (91 m) along the canyon walls and includes some 200 figures of humans and gods.

Native American Peoples

(Before European Contact)

This map shows the general area of Native American peoples before European settlers arrived.

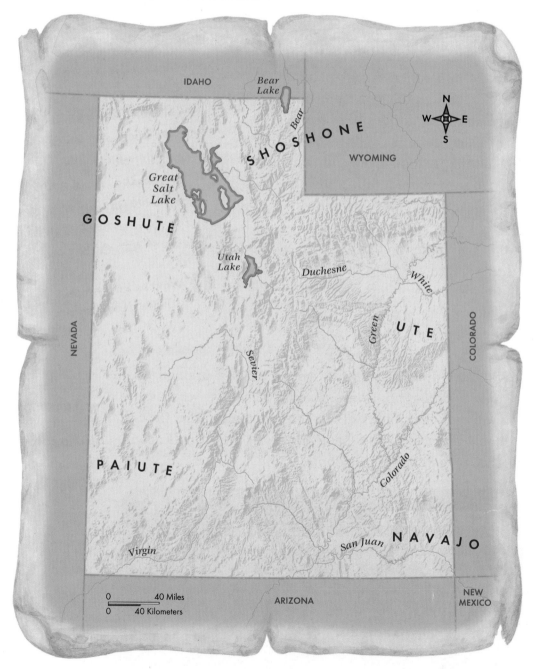

Ancestral Pueblo women grinding corn

THE ANCESTRAL PUEBLO PEOPLE

The Ancestral Pueblo people appeared sometime around 200 CE. The early Ancestral Pueblo people lived in pit houses—holes in the ground roofed with poles. They covered the poles with mats and mud. Sometimes they combined several pits to form a large structure that two or more families may have shared.

Several new inventions made life easier for the Ancestral Pueblo people. Instead of throwing spears, they hunted game with bows and arrows. They had learned to raise much of their own food by planting corn, beans, and squash, and they had domesticated turkeys that they raised for meat. They also knew how to make beautiful pottery vessels for storing food and water. And they began weaving exquisite baskets that were used for storage as well.

Ancestral Pueblo pottery

Picture Yourself . . .

as an Ancestral Pueblo on the Eve of Leaving

It is early morning. Outside on the terrace, the turkeys are gobbling, demanding to be fed. Your mother grinds corn on a flat stone, and your father is preparing to go hunting with some of the other men of your village. You hope they will come back with a deer or at least some rabbits. The corn this year is stunted and tough because there has been so little rain. Sometimes all you can think about is food, and there is never enough to fill you properly.

A lot of people are saying that it would be best to leave this place and move south. They say it rains more in the southern mountains, and it will be easier to raise crops. This is the only home you have ever known, and you feel like crying when you think of going away. You would miss this village and your home on the cliffside. You would miss the morning sounds of turkeys and grinding stones. No one can tell you what life would be like in the new land.

WORD TO KNOW

famine *a period of extreme food shortages and hunger*

Q8 WHAT IS THE DIFFERENCE BETWEEN A PICTOGRAPH AND A PETROGLYPH?

A8 A pictograph is a painting on stone. A petroglyph is a picture that is carved into stone by chipping away with tools.

Over the centuries, the Ancestral Pueblo people began to build stone houses above the ground. They used pit houses for religious ceremonies. By around 1100, they were living in stone houses in large villages. Many of the houses were built into cliffs.

Sometime around 1250, the Ancestral Pueblo people abandoned their villages in the Four Corners region, seeming to have left in a great hurry. They walked away from bowls and baskets as though they expected to be back in only a few days, but they never returned. They moved south into today's New Mexico and Arizona, where some of their descendants still live as Pueblo Indians.

Why did the Ancestral Pueblo people abandon their cliff dwellings? Some scientists think that climate changes may have caused a sudden **famine**. Others believe that hostile neighbors drove them away. Nobody knows for sure. The abandonment of the Ancestral Pueblo cliff dwellings remains a mystery.

THE FREMONT PEOPLE

While the Ancestral Pueblo people were developing their civilization in the Four Corners, a group known today as the Fremont people lived on the Colorado Plateau and in eastern parts of the Basin and Range Province. In some places, the Fremont people were nomadic hunters. Other groups lived in settled villages. So what did the Fremont

Some Shoshonean people made their homes in Utah.

peoples have in common with one another? Their art-work. Fremont petroglyphs and pictographs show large, strong-looking people wearing necklaces and earrings. Clay figures of people and animals have also been found.

THE SHOSHONEAN PEOPLE

Sometime around 1300, bands of people from the south-west began moving into Utah. These people belonged to several groups that shared similar customs and spoke related languages. Scholars call them Shoshonean peo-ples. In Utah, Shoshoneans fall into four main groups: Shoshones in northern and northeastern Utah, Goshutes in the northwest, Southern Paiutes in the southwest, and Utes in central and eastern Utah.

Goshutes, or Gosiutes, and the Southern Paiute peoples lived in some of the driest, harshest regions of present-day Utah. The Goshute homeland was the

GRASSHOPPER ROUNDUP

Insects are a rich source of protein, and grasshoppers were a valuable source of food for Goshutes. An early European explorer described a full-scale grasshopper hunt: "They begin by digging a hole, ten or twelve feet [3 or 4 m] in diameter by four or five feet [1.2 or 1.5 m]; then, armed with long branches . . . they surround a field of four or five acres [1.6 or 2 ha]. . . . They stand about twenty feet [6 m] apart, and their whole work is to beat the ground, so as to frighten up the grasshoppers and make them bound forward. They chase them toward the center, into the hole. . . . Frequently three or four acres [1.2 or 1.6 ha] furnish grasshoppers to fill the hole."

During certain ceremonies, Utes put glittering quartz crystals in a skin rattle. When the rattle was shaken, the crystals flashed like magical bits of starlight.

southern portion of Great Salt Lake Desert and the Deep Creek Mountains along today's Utah–Nevada border. The Southern Paiute people lived farther south.

For Goshutes and Southern Paiutes, life was a never-ending search for food. In summer, they gathered the nuts of the piñon pine, which they stored for the winter when other foods were scarce. They also hunted rabbits, birds, and pronghorn.

Goshutes and Southern Paiutes moved from place to place in small family groups. Sometimes they lived in caves, and at times they built shelters called wickiups from branches. There were no hereditary chiefs or rulers, but groups did choose wise men who offered advice and helped lead the community. Occasionally, several bands met to hunt rabbits or pronghorn.

Shoshones and Utes were skilled hunters. Like Goshutes and Southern Paiutes, they sometimes joined forces to hunt rabbits, antelope, and other game. They also gathered roots, berries, wild fruit, and edible seeds. They moved often and lived in cone-shaped tents called tipis. The tipi was made of poles leaning together at the top and covered with brush or animal skins. A tipi was usually 15 to 20 feet (4.6 to 6 m) across at the base. A whole family could sleep snugly inside.

One or more leaders led the Ute and Shoshone bands. Another important member of the group was the shaman, or healer. Shamans treated disease by chanting spells to drive the illness out of the person's body. Shoshones and Utes also knew about hundreds of plants that had healing powers.

Utes and Shoshones sometimes attacked neighboring villages. In peacetime, they gathered for dances to celebrate the seasons. The Bear Dance, held each summer, lasted for ten days. Men and women danced all day to the beat of drums and the music of flutes. In the evening,

These Utes are shown wearing traditional clothing.

people told stories and played games of chance. In one game, a man held a stone in his fist. People placed bets as to which hand held the stone.

WHAT TO WEAR?

For the Indians of Utah, clothing was simple and practical. Women wore skirts of deerskin or fabric woven from yucca strips and strips of rabbit skin. Men wore leather **breechcloths**. In winter, men and women draped blankets around their shoulders. Shoshones and Utes wore moccasins made of rabbit skin with the fur on the inside. Goshutes and Southern Paiutes made moccasins from yucca strips.

WORD TO KNOW

breechcloths *garments worn by men over their lower bodies*

THE CREATION OF UTES

According to the Ute people, the Great Spirit, Senatahv, created many plants and animals to live on the earth. One day, he cut some sticks and put them in a sack. Coyote, the trickster, opened the bag and found that the sticks had turned into people. He let most of the people out, and they scattered around the earth, speaking in many different tongues. When Senatahv saw what Coyote had done, he was angry. He said the scattered people would fight many wars over land. Only one group of people was left in the sack. Senatahv took them out and made them especially strong and brave. These people became Utes.

Many Navajo people lived in homes like this one. They were made of mud and sticks, and the doors usually faced east.

UNDERSTANDING THE WORLD

Like people everywhere, the Indians of Utah tried to understand the world they lived in. They believed that spirits lived in the plants and animals around them and even in the rocks, clouds, sun, and moon. The wolf was the most sacred animal to Shoshones. Utes especially honored the spirit of the bear. All Indian groups in Utah saw the coyote as a trickster god who brought mischief into the world. Every group told stories about Coyote and his troublesome ways.

THE NAVAJO PEOPLE ARRIVE

The Navajo people, or Dine, were the last Native Americans to settle in present-day Utah. They originated in western Canada and reached the Southwest around 1620. As they spread into Utah and surrounding areas, Navajos sometimes battled other groups. At the same time, they adopted many of the beliefs and customs of the southwestern Indians. They quickly learned to live in the dry desert climate. The Navajo people became one of the most powerful Indian groups in the West.

HOOFBEATS IN THE MOUNTAINS

In the 1500s, Spaniards brought horses to the Americas. Sometime in the 1600s, Utes and Shoshones obtained their first horses. They may have come from Spanish settlements in New Mexico or from Native groups to the south and the east.

Horses dramatically changed life for Utes and Shoshones who owned them. The people quickly became highly skilled riders. Hunters on horseback could chase and kill bison and other game. Mounted warriors could attack neighbors and rove far from home to raid enemy villages. Some families grew wealthy by owning many horses.

The horse transformed life for the Indians. But far greater changes were still to come.

Shoshones and other Native groups began using horses after Spanish explorers brought the animals to the Americas.

READ ABOUT

European explorers and American pioneers faced tough terrain such as Bryce Canyon when they journeyed through Utah.

1776

The Domínguez-
Escalante expedition
sets out for Utah
from Santa Fe

1822 ▸

James Henry Ashley
forms the Ashley
Company to trap
animals and trade furs
in Utah

Beaver fur hat

1828

An exploring party
proves that Great
Salt Lake is not
part of the Pacific
Ocean

CHAPTER THREE

EXPLORATION AND SETTLEMENT

★

IN 1765, JUAN ANTONIO RIVERA LED A SMALL EXPEDITION FROM NEW MEXICO AS FAR WEST AS PRESENT-DAY MOAB. At a shallow spot on the Colorado River, he set a wooden cross with an inscription, claiming the territory for Spain. The Spanish government had learned of English traders on the coast of what is now Oregon. To fend off the British, Spain wanted to strengthen its presence across the region.

1841

Nancy and Ann Kelsey become the first white females to cross the Utah desert

1845 ►

John C. Frémont publishes a report on his explorations in Utah

1847

Brigham Young leads a party of Mormons to Salt Lake Valley

European Exploration of Utah

The colored arrows on this map show the routes taken by explorers and pioneers between 1776 and 1823.

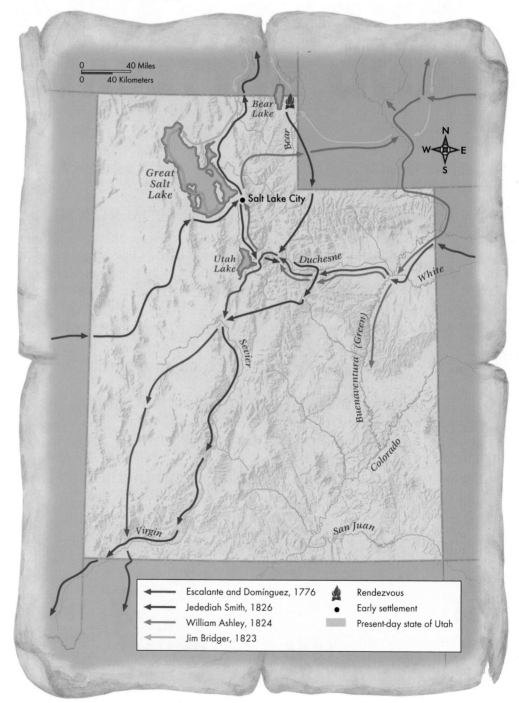

Escalante and Domínguez, 1776		Rendezvous
Jedediah Smith, 1826		Early settlement
William Ashley, 1824		Present-day state of Utah
Jim Bridger, 1823		

The Domínguez-Escalante expedition relied on Ute guides when they traveled through the Utah Valley.

SPANISH EXPEDITIONS

Spanish exploration pushed deeper into Utah in 1776, when Francisco Atanasio Domínguez and Silvestre Vélez de Escalante arrived there. They hoped to find a route to California from Santa Fe in New Mexico. Along the way, they planned to convert Native Americans to Christianity.

Domínguez and Escalante traveled as far as the Green River near today's Dinosaur National Monument. Along the way, they met a group of Utes, whom they gave new Spanish names. Two of the Indians, a young man they called Silvestre and a 12-year-old boy they called Joaquin, agreed to guide them into the Utah Valley.

Picture Yourself...

as a Ute Child Greeting European Explorers

Ever since you were small, you have heard stories about the strange pale-skinned people who live far to the south. Once, your father returned from hunting and brought a knife so hard and strong that no stone could break it. He said it came from the white men and said that your people should trade with them for knives and other wonderful things.

Now white men on horses have come to your village. You peer shyly from your hut and watch every move they make. They want to travel north, and they ask some of your people to guide them. Your uncle agrees to go and tells your brother to go, too. Your brother looks scared, but you can tell he's excited. The strangers seem kind, but you're frightened to think of your brother going so far away with them. You wonder if you will ever see him again.

Utes told the Spaniards that a huge lake lay to the north. In his journal, Escalante wrote that "[Its waters] are harmful and extremely salty, for the [Indians] assured us that anyone who wet some part of his body with them immediately felt a lot of itching in the part moistened." Domínguez and Escalante did not try to find this mysterious lake. Early snows had begun to fall, and they decided to return to Santa Fe with their maps and their stories.

Domínguez and Escalante recorded no traces of English settlement in the country they had seen. Their map suggested that a river, which they called the Buenaventura, flowed into the Laguna de Miera, a small salt lake that was later called Sevier Lake.

The Spaniards sent a few more expeditions to explore the country of the Ute people, but with limited success. Spain was weakening, and the great Spanish empire in the Americas was starting to crumble. In 1821, Mexico revolted against Spanish rule and became an independent nation. Mexico claimed all of the territory as far north as Utah. But it did not have the resources to establish settlements on its northern frontier, so Utah was Mexican in name only.

The United States was a young nation, and it was growing quickly. Settlers were carving new states out of the territory east of the Mississippi River and starting to look westward. Some politicians began to claim that God intended the United States to stretch from the Atlantic Coast to the Pacific Ocean. They called their idea Manifest Destiny.

A fur trader's boat is piled with animal pelts on the Bear River, mid-1800s.

ON THE TRAIL OF THE BEAVER

In March 1822, an American businessman named William Henry Ashley ran a notice in a St. Louis newspaper. The notice was addressed "To Enterprising Young Men" and said that Ashley wished "to engage one hundred young men to ascend the Missouri River to its source, there to be employed for one, two, or three years." He was planning to establish a company to trap beavers and other fur-bearing animals in the Rocky Mountains. To his delight, his ad brought hundreds of replies. Soon he had all the recruits he needed.

In the years that followed, the men of Ashley's company spread across present-day Colorado, Utah, Wyoming, and Idaho. As they trapped and traded with the various Native American nations, they mapped the western lands.

The men of Ashley's company were not the only trappers in the Rockies. There were French Canadians, Mexicans, and British. James P. Beckwourth, an African

Native Americans brought furs to trading posts like this one.

THE HEIGHT OF FASHION

In the early decades of the 19th century, all fashionable people in England and France wore beaver-fur hats. To feed the market for pelts, beavers in eastern North America had been trapped nearly to extinction. In the Rocky Mountains and the Pacific Northwest, however, the supply of beavers and other fur-bearing animals seemed inexhaustible. The glossy pelt of the beaver led whites to explore much of the West.

A hat made of beaver fur

American born in Virginia, became a noted frontier trader, explorer, and guide. He was trapping in the Utah region by 1825, and he frequented the area over the next few years.

The Hudson's Bay Company, a British business, competed with Ashley's men for trade with the Indians of the Rockies. For a short time, Peter Skene Ogden of the Hudson's Bay Company tried to set up trade in Utah. Ashley's men drove him out and took control of the Utah territory.

The early trappers, or mountain men, were adventurous. They knew how to survive in the mountains and forests, and often spent weeks or months alone. Some mastered the languages and customs of Utes and other Native Americans, and married Indian women.

Some historians believe that a mountain man named Etienne Provost was the first white person to see Great Salt

Lake. Provost may have reached the lake in the fall of 1824. Jim Bridger, an American mountain man, arrived at the salty lake in the spring of 1825. Bridger thought that the lake was an arm of the Pacific Ocean. Three years later, an exploring party tramped all the way around the lake and proved that it did not lead to the coast.

Mountain men established a few trading posts in Utah. Trapper and scout Kit Carson set up a post at the fork of the Green and White rivers in 1833. Fort Davy Crockett was established in 1837 on the Green River near the border with today's Colorado.

By the 1840s, the fur trade began to decline. Trappers had exhausted the supply

Settlers arriving at the Great Salt Lake, mid-1800s

MINI-BIO

JIM BRIDGER: PATHFINDER

At the age of 18, Jim Bridger (1804–1881) signed on as a fur trader with the Ashley Company. He had a remarkable talent for learning languages and mastered a dozen Indian tongues. He lived and worked as a mountain man for 20 years, traveling throughout the northern Rockies. In 1861, Bridger became a U.S. Army scout. His pathfinding skills helped open the way for western settlement.

❓ **Want to know more?** Visit www.factsfornow.scholastic.com and enter the keyword **Utah**.

MINI-BIO

JEDEDIAH SMITH: THE BIBLE AND THE GUN

Jedediah Smith (1799–1831) was born in New York. As a young man, he signed on with William Ashley's company and headed west to work as a trapper. Smith was different from most mountain men, who were sometimes rough and rowdy. People said that Smith traveled the trails with a gun in one hand and a Bible in the other. He made three bold journeys across the deserts of the Great Basin between Utah and California, with men of many races. He died at age 32 in a fight with Comanche Indians.

? Want to know more? Visit www.factsfornow .scholastic.com and enter the keyword **Utah**.

of beavers and other animals. The price for beaver pelts rose as they grew scarce. Then beaver hats became so expensive that they fell out of fashion. European gentlemen started to wear silk hats, and the mountain men gradually found other ways to make a living.

WESTWARD HO!

During the 1830s and 1840s, stories of rich lands along the Pacific reached the East Coast. From New England to the Midwest, farmers and adventurers dreamed of starting new lives in California or Oregon. Trappers had found South Pass, an easy route through the mountains in southern Wyoming that helped to open the way to Oregon. Soon strings of wagon trains rumbled west along a route known as the Oregon Trail.

In 1841, a party of settlers chose to leave the well-used trail and take a shortcut through Utah to California. Somehow word had never reached John Bartleson, the expedition's leader, that the Buenaventura River did not exist. He planned to follow the Buenaventura west from Great Salt Lake all the way to San Francisco Bay. Instead, the forlorn little wagon train—hot, thirsty, and desperate—struggled across the Great Salt Desert.

Among the members of the party were a young man named Benjamin Kelsey, his wife, Nancy, and their baby daughter, Ann. Nancy and Ann Kelsey became the first white females to cross Utah. Despite their hardships, the Bartleson–Bidwell Party finally stumbled into California's

San Joaquin Valley. The entire journey from Missouri to California took them six long months.

MARKING THE TRAIL

Between 1843 and 1854, John C. Frémont made multiple trips across Utah. The U.S. government paid him to draw maps and to make scientific measurements of Utah's lakes and mountains. In 1844, he and his exploring party climbed a small mountain for their first view of Great Salt Lake. "Ascending to the summit," he wrote, "immediately at our feet [we] beheld the object of our anxious search—the waters of the Inland Sea, stretching in still and solitary grandeur far beyond the limit of our vision."

On a later expedition, Frémont crossed the Great Basin and made his way to California. He recommended the Great Basin route as a good shortcut for wagons headed to California, "not only on account of the less distance, but . . . [because it is] less mountainous, with good pasturage and well watered." Frémont described the route to a California promoter named Lansford Hastings, who encouraged its use by westward-bound wagon trains. It became known as the Hastings Cutoff.

Explorer John C. Frémont made five journeys across Utah and created maps of the region.

John Frémont had many Utah firsts. He was the first person to make an accurate map of Great Salt Lake, and the first white person to visit its islands. He was the first person to measure the lake's depth and to do a scientific study of its water.

MINI-BIO

JOSEPH SMITH: A BOY AND A VISION

Joseph Smith (1805–1844) came from a poor, religious family. As a teenager, Smith said, he had a vision. In this vision, an angel led him to a hill near his family's New York farm and showed him a set of golden tablets that told the story of an ancient Christian kingdom in North America. Smith began preaching in nearby towns, winning converts wherever he went. In 1830, he published The Book of Mormon, his translation of the tablets. The book spread the new religion to thousands of people in the United States and Europe. But when Smith encouraged Mormon men to take more than one wife, outraged non-Mormons shot and killed him.

? **Want to know more?** Visit www.factsfornow .scholastic.com and enter the keyword **Utah**.

Frémont's report of his explorations was published in 1845. People all over the country read his descriptions of Utah Lake, Great Salt Lake, the Cache Valley, and other features of this little-known land in Mexico.

A NEW RELIGION

In 1830, Joseph Smith had founded the Church of Jesus Christ of Latter-day Saints (LDS), based on several visions he claimed to have had. Smith and his followers established a community at Kirtland, Ohio, but religious persecution forced them to leave first Ohio and then Nauvoo,

A Mormon wagon train passes through Echo Canyon, east of Salt Lake City.

Illinois. On June 27, 1844, an angry mob shot and killed Smith in Carthage, Illinois. Brigham Young, one of Smith's chief followers, quickly took command. He declared that the Latter-day Saints, or Mormons, must leave the United States.

THE JOURNEY TO ZION

In the fall of 1846, Brigham Young gathered some 10,000 of his followers on the banks of the Missouri River. At Winter Quarters, Nebraska, they prepared for the journey ahead. Meanwhile, thousands of other Mormons prepared to join the group. "We do not want one saint to be left in the United States," declared Mormon apostle Orson Pratt. In California and New England, and as far away as Mexico and Germany, the Latter-day Saints waited for instructions.

On April 16, 1847, Brigham Young set out from Winter Quarters with a well-trained advance band of 143 men (including three enslaved Africans), three women, and two children. Their mission was to select a site for the new settlement and make it ready for the church members who would follow. Young had studied Frémont's report with painstaking care. Frémont had written that Salt Lake Valley was "surrounded by lofty mountains . . . believed to be filled with rivers and lakes which have no communication with the sea, deserts and oases which have never been explored." Young added Utah to his list of possible sites, which also included California and Oregon.

MINI-BIO

ELIZA SNOW: GIVING STRENGTH TO THE MOVEMENT

Ohioan Eliza Snow (1804–1887) traveled to Utah and worked as a leader within the Mormon movement. In 1866, she became president of the Relief Society, an organization that improved opportunities for Mormon women. The society sent women to medical school, started the first hospital in Salt Lake City, and opened a granary for storing grain. Snow wrote many poems that were set to music as Mormon hymns and are sung to this day.

? Want to know more? Visit www.factsfornow.scholastic.com and enter the keyword **Utah**.

Brigham Young leading his followers on their journey to Salt Lake Valley in 1847

Q8 HOW DID THE PIONEERS MEASURE DISTANCES ON THE TRAIL?

A8 At first, Young ordered some of his men to count the number of times a wagon wheel turned. After three weeks, two members of the advance band built a machine that counted for them.

Like a military general, Young organized his followers into units of 50, broken again into squads of 10. Every day at 5:00 A.M., a bugle call wakened the camp. The emigrants had breakfast, hitched up their horses and mules, and set off by 8:00. They traveled all day and stopped to camp at 8:30 P.M. By 9:00, everyone was expected to be in bed, gathering strength for another day on the trail. Only Sunday was a day of rest. At this pace, the pioneers covered 15 to 20 miles (24 to 32 km) a day.

In July, several of the pioneers, including Brigham Young, fell ill with a fever. The sick members stopped to rest, and Orson Pratt led the remaining party forward. On July 21, he climbed Donner Hill and saw Mexico's Salt Lake Valley for the first time. Pratt wrote, "We could not refrain from a shout of joy . . . the moment this grand and lovely scenery was within our view."

The following day, Pratt and his band cut a trail that allowed wagons to roll into the valley. The next day, they unloaded their gear and set to work plowing the land. On July 24, Young and the others caught up with Pratt's party. From his wagon, Young watched the pioneers hard at work in the valley. Years later, one of his followers recalled his simple words of approval: "It is enough. This is the right place. Drive on."

A view of the settlement that the Mormon group founded in Salt Lake Valley

MINI-BIO

GREEN FLAKE: AFRICAN AMERICAN PIONEER

Enslaved African American Green Flake (1828–1903) drove Brigham Young's wagon at the head of the advance party of Mormon pioneers. In 1854, Flake was freed from slavery. He and his wife established a prosperous farm in the Salt Lake Valley. In 1897, he attended the Jubilee Pioneer Celebration in Salt Lake City. He was one of the last survivors of the Mormon trek of 1847. He received a certificate of honor, which he proudly hung in his home.

? **Want to know more?** Visit www.factsfornow .scholastic.com and enter the keyword **Utah.**

READ ABOUT

The Mormon Temple
in Temple Square
was constructed in
the late 1800s.

1850

Utah becomes a U.S.
territory

▲ 1856–60

Three thousand
Mormons migrate to
Utah as part of the
handcart brigade

1857

Mormons and Indians
kill 120 people in the
Mountain Meadows
Massacre

CHAPTER FOUR

GROWTH AND CHANGE

★

BRIGHAM YOUNG WAS NOT CONTENT TO FOUND A SIMPLE FRONTIER SETTLEMENT. He envisioned a magnificent city as the center of the Mormons' kingdom. One of his work crews laid out this city in 135 ten-acre (4 ha) blocks. At the center was the site for a great Mormon temple. Today, Temple Square is the centerpiece of Salt Lake City.

1865–72
Utes resist being forced onto reservations during the Black Hawk War

1869
The first transcontinental railroad is completed at Promontory, Utah

1896 ▶
Utah enters the Union as the 45th state

A GREAT THRIVING ORCHARD

In 1861, writer Mark Twain visited Salt Lake City on a journey across the West. He recounted these impressions in *Roughing It*: "Next day we strolled about everywhere through the broad, straight, level streets, and enjoyed the pleasant strangeness of a city of fifteen thousand inhabitants with no loafers perceptible in it; and no visible drunkards or noisy people; . . . block after block of trim dwellings, built of 'frame' and sunburned brick—a great thriving orchard and garden behind every one of them, . . . and a grand general air of neatness, repair, thrift and comfort, around and about and over the whole."

A Salt Lake City street in 1868

UNEASY NEIGHBORS

A few days after the Mormons arrived in Salt Lake Valley, a group of Shoshone Indians came to meet with Brigham Young. The Mormons were plowing territory where generations of Shoshones had hunted game, and the Indians were concerned. Young and the Shoshone leader agreed that they would try to live peacefully as neighbors.

The Mormons believed that the Indians had descended from the Lost Tribes of Israel described in the Book of Mormon. They felt it was their mission to convert the Native Americans to the Mormon faith and to teach them to farm the land. The Indians resisted the settlers' ideas and beliefs. Conflicts flared as Mormon settlements spread through Salt Lake Valley and into the land to the south. The Walker War in 1853 was a series of clashes in which the Ute people tried to preserve their ancient ways and lands from the encroaching Mormons.

THE STRUGGLE FOR SURVIVAL

The Mormons' first winter in Utah was mild, and the community flourished. When the days began to get longer, the farmers planted their fields once more. All seemed to be going well when suddenly, toward the end of May, swarms of crickets descended. Harriet Young, one of Brigham Young's many wives, wrote in her journal, "They have destroyed ¾ of an acre [0.3 ha] of squashes, two acres [0.8 ha] of millet and our rye, and are now to work in our wheat."

Before the crickets could do their worst, a huge flock of gulls rose from an island in Great Salt Lake. The white-winged birds swept down on the fields and devoured the munching hordes. To the Mormons, the arrival of the gulls was a miracle. It seemed to prove that God wanted them to succeed.

SEE IT HERE!

THE SALT LAKE TEMPLE

The Salt Lake Temple stands at the center of Temple Square. Construction of this temple began in 1853 and was completed 40 years later in 1893. The temple is 186 feet (57 m) long and 118 feet (36 m) wide. The walls are 9 feet (2.7 m) thick at the base and 6 feet (1.8 m) thick at the top. Its tallest spire reaches 210 feet (64 m) into the air. On one of the temple's six spires stands a 12½-foot (3.8 m) statue of the angel said to have inspired Mormon founder Joseph Smith. It is made of copper covered with gold leaf.

MINI-BIO

WAKARA: LEGENDARY LEADER

Wakara (c. 1808–1855) was a powerful Ute leader from the Spanish Fork River region in southern Utah. During the 1840s, Wakara led raids on trading caravans and settlements from Utah to California. For a time, he encouraged peaceful relations with the Mormons in Utah, who called him Walker and baptized him into the LDS Church in 1850. But as settlers continued to push into Ute territory, Wakara ultimately fought back.

Want to know more? Visit www.factsfornow.scholastic.com and enter the keyword **Utah**.

WORD TO KNOW

arable *capable of being farmed, tillable*

THE HANDCART BRIGADES

In 1856, Brigham Young began a program that he hoped would provide an inexpensive way for emigrants to reach Utah. He arranged for parties of settlers to travel by pushing handcarts loaded with their household goods. Each handcart weighed several hundred pounds. Between 1856 and 1860, about 3,000 handcart emigrants made their way to Utah. Handcart pioneers made up only a fraction of the Mormons who moved to Utah, but they left an enduring mark on Utah history.

Mormons crossing the plains with a handcart on the way to Utah in the mid-1800s

THE WIDENING KINGDOM

When the first tasks were completed, Young and some of the advance party returned to Winter Quarters to fetch another group of settlers. Mormons arrived from California, Texas, the Midwest, and other locations as well. **Arable** land in the Salt Lake Valley was in short supply, and soon it had all been parceled out. New settlements sprang up anywhere that had enough water to nourish crops.

The town of Bountiful was founded in 1848. The following year, the Mormons started the towns of Ogden, Provo, Tooele, and Manti. In general, they settled first along the western side of the Wasatch Range, where the most desirable land was found. Later, they pushed into more and more remote areas. Not all of the settlers went to remote locations by choice. Often their leaders assigned them to go.

BECOMING AMERICAN

When Brigham Young reached the Salt Lake Valley in 1847, Utah belonged to Mexico, which was still smarting from Texas's successful fight for independence. Now the United States wanted more Mexican lands, and it was willing to wage the Mexican-American War for them.

As more people moved to Utah Territory, towns were created in the mountainous landscape.

In February 1848, Mexico lost the war and half of its territory. Under the Treaty of Guadalupe Hidalgo, the United States gained a huge stretch of land that included present-day Arizona, California, New Mexico, and parts of Colorado, Nevada, and Utah. The Mormons had moved to Utah to escape persecution in the United States. Now they were living on land that belonged to the U.S. government once more.

The situation was unavoidable, and Brigham Young tried to make the best of it. If the kingdom was to be part of the United States, he reasoned, then it should apply to become an official U.S. territory. Territorial status would be a step toward statehood. Statehood would allow the Mormons to elect their own officials and basically govern themselves.

UTAH TERRITORY

At first, Utah Territory included an immense sweep of land. It stretched from western Colorado to Nevada. In 1861, Utah Territory was carved up into the territories of Nevada, Utah, and Colorado. Other pieces were later chipped away to become part of Wyoming. Utah arrived at its present boundaries in 1868.

FAQ

Q8 WHAT IS THE DIFFERENCE BETWEEN A STATE AND A TERRITORY?

A8 In a territory, the federal government appoints many governing officials. Citizens of a territory do not have voting representatives in Congress and cannot vote in national elections. Citizens of a state vote for their own state officials and also vote in national elections. States elect voting senators and representatives to Congress.

THE QUESTION OF SLAVERY

A number of white Mormons from Southern states brought enslaved African Americans with them to Utah. Some free African Americans who had become Mormons also moved to Utah. By 1850, 26 enslaved and 24 free African American men, women, and children lived in Utah Territory. Despite the African American contribution to Mormon migrations and settlements, church elders continued to approve of slavery. Brigham Young personally refused to become a master, but he said his colony could not prosper without enslaved workers, and he welcomed slaveholders to Salt Lake City.

In 1852, Utah passed a law that made slavery legal in the territory. Congress overturned this law in 1862. When Congress declared slavery illegal in U.S. territories, many newly freed African Americans left Utah to start new lives in California and Oregon.

In 1850, the Mormons sent a petition to Washington, D.C., asking to be recognized as the territory of Deseret. The petition bore 2,270 signatures and measured 22 feet (7 m) long! Congress rejected the name Deseret but it did create the Territory of Utah. President Millard Fillmore appointed Brigham Young to serve as the first territorial governor. The capital city, located in the middle of the territory, was named Fillmore in the president's honor. Utah's capital moved to Salt Lake City in 1855.

UTAH AT WAR

In the years that followed, U.S. presidents tried to appoint non-Mormon governors to Utah Territory. These governors and other officials met strong resistance from Brigham Young and his followers. The Mormons wanted to govern themselves without interference from Washington. "I am and will be Governor," declared Young at one public meeting, "and no power can hinder it until the Lord Almighty says, 'Brigham, you need not be Governor any longer.'"

Meanwhile, in the eastern United States, fierce anti-Mormon feelings brewed. With their church-based government, the Mormons defied the separation between church and state that the U.S. Constitution required. Furthermore, their practice of **polygamy** was distressing to many Americans. Mormon Utah seemed a threat to some of the basic beliefs in American society.

A U.S. Army supply train crossing the Utah plains

A magazine editorial in April 1857 proclaimed, "At whatever cost, the United States must declare its supremacy."

In 1857, President James Buchanan appointed a non-Mormon from Georgia, Alfred Cumming, to be Utah's next governor. Fearing that the Mormons would rebel, Buchanan sent Cumming west with a military escort. When the Mormons learned that soldiers were marching into their territory, they prepared for war.

As the army drew nearer, a wagon train from Arkansas crossed Utah on its way to California. The Fancher Train, as it was called, stopped for supplies in the Utah town of Cedar City. Brigham Young had ordered the Mormons not to sell food to travelers because all supplies were needed for the conflict ahead. When the people of Cedar City refused to sell them any food, the people in the Fancher Train grew angry. According to some accounts, a few of

WORD TO KNOW

polygamy *the practice of having two or more spouses at the same time*

the men threatened to rally an army in California and send it back to Utah to fight Brigham Young and his people.

The Fancher Train left Cedar City and camped at Mountain Meadows, some 35 miles (56 km) away. There unfolded one of the most shameful incidents in Utah history. A band of Mormons and a few Native Americans surrounded the wagons and persuaded the men of the Fancher Train to lay down their guns. Then they attacked the unarmed travelers. Altogether they killed 120 men, women, and children. The attackers spared only 17 of the youngest children, those under six years old. One man, John D. Lee, was convicted of murder 20 years after the massacre occurred. He was executed at the site where the murders took place. No one else was ever convicted.

In 1858, Brigham Young decided that his people could not resist a military invasion. Instead of fighting, they

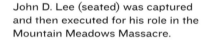

John D. Lee (seated) was captured and then executed for his role in the Mountain Meadows Massacre.

gathered their belongings, boarded up their houses, and abandoned Salt Lake City. Mormons from far-flung settlements also took flight. In all, as many as 40,000 people left their homes and farms and headed south to Provo.

Colonel Albert Johnston led U.S. troops during the so-called Utah War. Two representatives from President Buchanan negotiated peace with the Mormons before the army arrived in Utah, however. Under this agreement, the soldiers were to be installed some distance from Salt Lake City. After arriving in the Salt Lake Valley and camping west of the city, Johnston and his scouts decided to locate in Cedar Valley at what became Camp Floyd. The Mormons returned and picked up their lives where they had left off.

In 1861, the American Civil War began after 11 Southern states seceded, or withdrew, from the Union. The federal government called most of the troops from Fort Floyd to fight with the Union army. Colonel Patrick Connor was sent to Utah to keep an eye on the Mormons and the Indians.

Connor's idea of keeping peace with the Indians was to kill them off. In 1863, he led an attack on a Shoshone village at Bear River, just north of Utah's present-day boundary with Idaho. In one of the lowest points in U.S. military history, Connor and his men massacred about 250 Shoshones, including 90 women and children.

MINI-BIO

ANN ELIZA WEBB YOUNG: WIFE NUMBER 19

In 1868, Ann Eliza Webb (1844–1878) married Brigham Young. She was miserable as a **plural wife** and divorced him. She gave lectures all over the United States about the conditions faced by plural wives. In 1875, she published a book called *Wife No. 19, or The Story of a Life in Bondage: Being a Complete Exposé of Mormonism, and Revealing the Sorrows, Sacrifices and Sufferings of Women in Polygamy.* The book fanned anti-Mormon feeling in the eastern United States.

? Want to know more? Visit www.factsfornow.scholastic.com and enter the keyword **Utah**.

WORD TO KNOW

plural wife *a woman whose husband has more than one wife at the same time*

EMPEROR OF MONUMENT VALLEY

In 1863, federal troops under Colonel Kit Carson attacked Navajos in Utah and Arizona. Hundreds of Navajos died during this campaign, but a band of 17 escaped, led by 35-year-old Hoskaninni (1828?–1912). In 1869, Hoskaninni's people came out of hiding and moved into Monument Valley along the border with Arizona. He discovered a source of silver in the mountains, and the band became rich.

In 1864, the U.S. government ordered the Utes of southern Utah to move to the Uintah Reservation in the valley of the Uinta River. Antonga Black Hawk led many of his people in armed resistance. The Black Hawk War, as it was called, was a series of clashes between Utes and whites from 1865 to 1872. Weakened by hunger and disease, the Utes finally were forced to settle on the reservation. Although treaties promised that the Utes would be paid for their land, the government never sent any payment.

CONNECTIONS WITH THE WORLD

In April 1860, the thunder of hooves signaled an end to Utah's isolation. For the next year and a half, wiry young Pony Express riders galloped east and west across the territory. The Pony Express carried pouches stuffed with mail from St. Joseph, Missouri, to Sacramento, California. Until then, Utah settlers had to wait months for a letter from back east. Tucked in a Pony Express saddlebag, a letter could travel from St. Joseph to Salt Lake City in only a week!

The Pony Express did not last long. It was replaced in 1861 after the completion of the first transcontinental telegraph line. Telegraph operators in stations along the line tapped out messages in Morse code. With lightning speed, news reached Utah from as far away as New York or Washington, D.C.

Pony Express rider

Chinese workers helped build the
Central Pacific Railroad in the 1860s.

In 1863, two crews of railroad workers began laying down tracks for a railroad that would span the United States from coast to coast. The Union Pacific Railroad Company, with crews of Irish workers, headed west from St. Joseph. Chinese workers for the Central Pacific Railroad Company hammered their way east from Sacramento. African Americans worked on both lines. The two railroad crews met at Promontory, Utah, on May 10, 1869. Crowds gathered for the ceremonial hammering of the golden spike that marked the completion of the transcontinental railroad.

Utah had rich mineral deposits. Gold, silver, lead, and coal had all been discovered. The railroads helped Utah begin large-scale mining operations by bringing in miners and carrying away loads of ore.

More and more, Utahns looked toward the world outside. And more and more, the world flooded into the territory. Some of the Irish and Chinese railroad workers stayed to make their homes in Utah's valleys. Italian and Welsh people arrived to take jobs in the mines. Many of these newcomers found themselves opposing Mormon authority and rules. They set up their own churches and demanded public schools for their children.

Utah sent petitions to Congress six times, asking for statehood. Each time, the request was turned down. Congress refused to grant statehood to Utah until polygamy was outlawed. In 1890, the LDS Church decreed that polygamy would no longer be permitted. Existing plural marriages could continue, but no such marriages would be performed in the future. On January 4, 1896, Utah became the 45th state to join the Union.

A store in Salt Lake City is decorated to celebrate Utah's statehood.

Utah: From Territory to Statehood

(1850–1896)

This map shows the original Utah territory and the area (in yellow) that became the state of Utah in 1896.

OREGON 1859

IDAHO 1890

WYOMING 1890

Spanish Treaty Line, 1819

Humboldt

Sacramento

Great Salt Lake

Green

Utah Territory, 1850

COLORADO 1876

NEVADA 1864

UTAH 1896

San Joaquin

San Juan

CALIFORNIA 1850

Colorado

Arizona Territory (until 1912)

New Mexico Territory (until 1912)

Rio Grande

PACIFIC OCEAN

Salt

Gila

TEXAS 1845

Gadsden Purchase, (To United States from Mexico, 1853)

MEXICO

Gulf of California

Ceded to United States by Mexico, 1848

U.S. territories

States

Utah, 1896

Purchased by United States, 1853

Utah Territory, 1850

N W E S

0   100 Miles
0   100 Kilometers

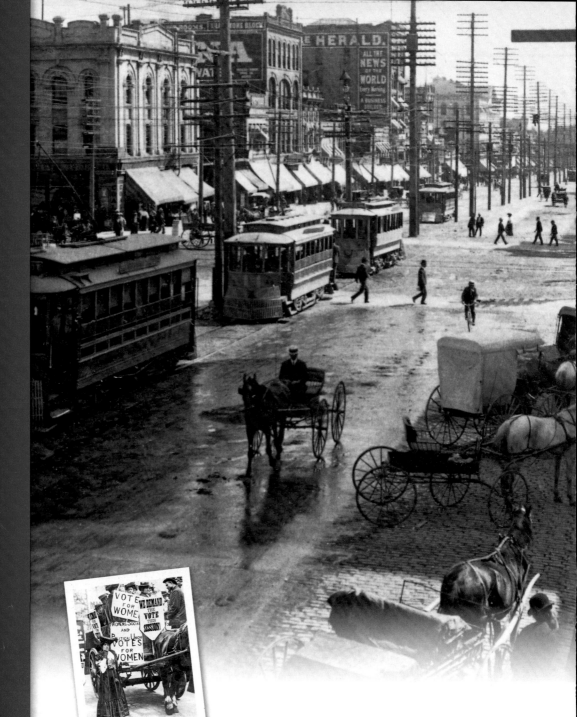

62

Streetcars and
carriages line
Main Street in Salt
Lake City, 1904.

1896 ▲

*Utah grants women
the right to vote
in state and local
elections*

1898

*More than 7 million Americans
sign a petition asking Congress
not to seat Utah representative
Brigham Roberts because he
has plural wives*

1913

*The Strawberry Dam
is built, providing
water to Utah's
deserts*

CHAPTER FIVE

MORE MODERN TIMES

★

AS THE 20TH CENTURY BEGAN, A SALT LAKE CITY RESIDENT WROTE A DESCRIPTION OF A NEW YEAR'S PARADE. He described the floats, the booming brass band, and the huge Chinese dragon. Thousands of Chinese people lived in Utah. So did people from Japan, Italy, Greece, and a dozen or more other countries. As it embarked upon statehood, Utah was becoming a medley of languages and cultures.

1942–45
Japanese Americans are held at Topaz Relocation Center near Delta

1950s
The U.S. military begins testing nuclear weapons in the Utah desert

2013 ▸
A light-rail extension opens from downtown Salt Lake City to the airport

Reed L. Smoot was elected to the U.S. Senate in 1902.

Martha Hughes Cannon

ACCEPTANCE AND CHANGE

Even after Congress accepted Utah's bid for statehood, many Americans viewed the area with suspicion. They feared that the LDS Church would control the way people voted and thought throughout the state. They also mistrusted Utah's history of polygamy. In 1898, Utahns elected Brigham H. Roberts, a man with several wives, to serve in the U.S. House of Representatives. More than 7 million Americans signed a petition calling on Congress to refuse to let Roberts serve. Congress voted to expel Roberts. Turmoil erupted again when Reed L. Smoot, a member of the LDS Church, was elected to the Senate in 1902. For four years, Smoot fought through the courts until he was finally allowed to take his Senate seat in 1907.

Women took an active role in early state politics. In 1896, a woman named Martha Hughes Cannon ran against her own husband for a seat in the state senate. She won the election, becoming the first female state senator in the nation! In 1912, Mary Woolley Chamberlain became mayor of Kanab and presided over an all-woman town council. It was the first all-female town council in the nation's history.

VOICES FROM MANY NATIONS

Many white settlers resented the Chinese who came to Utah to work on the railroads. White workers claimed that the Chinese pulled down wages because they were willing to work for low pay. White workers discriminated against the Chinese because of their unfamiliar language, style of dress, and religious beliefs.

In 1882, the U.S. Congress passed the Chinese Exclusion Act, closing the door to any further Chinese immigration. After the act took effect, Japanese immigration increased. In Utah, many Japanese immigrants worked on railroad crews or farms, especially in the sugar beet fields.

By the beginning of the 20th century, millions of newcomers from southern and eastern Europe were pouring into the United States. Some were recruited to work on the railroads in Utah and other western states. Others went to Utah to take jobs in the coal and copper mines and in the roaring factories where ore was smelted. In the late 1890s, groups of Italian workers settled in Utah's Carbon County. The Denver and Rio Grande Railroad hired them as maintenance workers or put them to work in coal mines to supply fuel for the engines. Serbians, Croatians, and Slovenes (all generally known as Slavic people) settled around Bingham, Murray, and Midvale. Immigrants from Greece worked in Carbon County's coal and copper mines.

Until 1920, women were not allowed to vote in national elections. But several western states gave women the vote much earlier. In Utah Territory, women were allowed to vote from 1870 until 1887, when Congress made it illegal. Then, in 1896, Utah became one of the first states to allow women to vote in state and local elections.

At first, most immigrants to Utah were young men. Later, they bought passage for their wives and others to join them in the new land. Small ethnic communities sprang up in Carbon and Bingham counties. Ogden and Salt Lake City developed Greek, Italian, Slavic, and Japanese neighborhoods. By 1910, 17 percent of all Utahns were foreign born. By 1920, roughly half of Utah's half million people were Mormons.

FARMING THE LAND

In 1913, the U.S. Bureau of Land Reclamation completed a dam on the Strawberry River, forming the Strawberry Reservoir. The reservoir brought water from the Colorado River Basin to the dry Great Basin in western Utah, creating thousands of acres of new farmland. Strawberry Dam was the first in a series of federal projects that provided water to **irrigate** Utah's deserts.

Irrigation was not the only method for extending Utah's agricultural regions. In the first decades of the 20th century, Utahns experimented with a technique called dryland farming. Farmers planted fields every other year. During the unplanted year, enough moisture built up in the soil so that the next year, a healthy crop could grow.

MINERS AND UNIONS

Working conditions for Utah's miners, mostly immigrants, were highly dangerous. Between 1914 and 1929, the number of deaths in Utah coal mine disasters was almost double the average nationwide.

In 1914, the Greek government sent Ambassador Maria Economidou to investigate the conditions of the state's Greek coal miners. She toured a mine near Clear Water and sent home a report on what she saw. She described traveling 3 miles (5 km) down a dark tunnel to a chamber deep

PERJURY FARM

During the 1880s, David Broadhead, a farmer from Nephi, was charged with **perjury** for claiming that he could grow wheat without irrigation. Broadhead went on to become one of the leading wheat growers in Utah, entirely through the use of dryland farming. He hung up a sign on his gate that read: "Perjury Farm."

WORDS TO KNOW

perjury *lying under oath in court*

irrigate *water land by artificial means to promote plant growth*

Stonecutters split granite boulders in Cottonwood Canyon for use in building the Mormon Tabernacle.

within the earth, where she found a crew of Greek men standing knee-deep in icy water. The air was foul with coal dust, and the men worked without rest, slamming their pickaxes at the chamber wall. Outraged, Economidou went to the mine owner and demanded better conditions for the workers. To her amazement, he insisted that the men liked their situation and didn't want it to change.

In 1903, Italian and Slavic coal miners in Carbon County went on **strike**, demanding higher wages and safer working conditions. The mine owners brought in Greek laborers to replace the striking miners. In 1912, miners from an assortment of ethnic backgrounds—Italians, Greeks, Slavs, and Japanese—walked off the job at the Bingham Canyon copper mine. This time, the mine operators broke the strike by bringing in Mexican workers.

WORD TO KNOW

strike *an organized refusal to work, usually as a sign of protest about working conditions*

THE SCOFIELD MINE DISASTER

On May 1, 1900, an explosion ripped through the Number Four coal mine near Scofield, operated by the Pleasant Valley Coal Company. Some 200 men and boys were killed by the blast or died from breathing poisonous gases that were released in the tunnels. The tragedy inspired a mournful folk song:

Oh, mothers and wives of the miners,
Who perished so suddenly there,
Did you give them a loving embrace that morn,
Did you bid them "Goodbye" with a prayer?

MINI-BIO

JOE HILL: THE SINGING MARTYR

Songwriter Joe Hill (1879–1915) drifted across the western states, working at an assortment of jobs. Many of his songs were about workers and their need to fight for their rights. In 1915, he was accused of murder. Despite flimsy evidence, he was convicted and sentenced to death. People all over the world rallied in his support, convinced that he had been framed because of his IWW involvement. Hill died before a firing squad in Salt Lake City. In a parting letter to an IWW leader he wrote, "Don't waste any time in mourning. Organize!"

 Want to know more? Visit www.factsfornow .scholastic.com and enter the keyword **Utah**.

Mine workers realized that the owners were playing one ethnic group against another. To fight for better conditions, thousands of miners joined **unions** that could make demands and bargain with management. Coal miners joined the United Mine Workers, and copper and lead miners became members of the Western Federation of Miners. Some miners became involved with the Industrial Workers of the World (IWW), an organization that argued that workers should run the mines and the government.

WAR AND HARD TIMES

In 1917, the United States entered World War I, a massive conflict that began in Europe in 1914. Thousands of young men from Utah put on uniforms and were shipped overseas to the battlefields. Their willingness to enlist helped

WORD TO KNOW

unions *organizations formed by workers to improve working conditions and wages*

assure the last doubters that Utah was indeed a state loyal to the U.S. government. Utah's mines provided much of the copper and lead needed for building weapons and other military supplies.

During the years after the war, which ended in 1918, prices for farm produce, coal, and copper tumbled. Mines cut their shifts or closed altogether. Many Utahns fell on hard times. White American soldiers returned home in search of jobs, and found themselves competing for work with African Americans and new immigrants. Many white Utahns took out their frustrations on blacks and immigrants.

Utah soldiers on an army transport vehicle in 1916

MASKED TERROR

The Ku Klux Klan, a white supremacist group, emerged in the South after the Civil War. The Klan terrorized African Americans who dared to exercise their right to vote, which they had won in the war. In Utah, the Klan also opposed Catholic immigrants and Asians. During the 1920s, the Klan gained considerable power in many parts of the country. The LDS Church did not support Klan activities and worked hard to prevent the Klan's hatred and violence from gaining ground in Utah.

WORD TO KNOW

stock *shares in the ownership of a company*

Groups such as the American Legion and the Ku Klux Klan (KKK) encouraged anti-foreign and anti-black feelings. The American Legion worked to shut down foreign-language newspapers and radio broadcasts. The Klan threatened the lives of immigrants and African Americans. In Salt Lake City, Magna, and Helper, Klan members attacked Greek shopkeepers and Greek men who were seen with "American" women. In 1925, Klansmen hanged an African American man named Robert Marshall near the town of Price.

In 1919, African Americans founded a branch of the National Association for the Advancement of Colored People (NAACP) in Salt Lake City. The NAACP and other organizations fought to eliminate the barriers of discrimination that kept black people from taking part fully in community life.

As Utah struggled economically in the 1920s, other parts of the country were booming. Prosperous visitors started traveling to scenic places in Utah. Tourism turned Utah's natural wonders into hard cash.

In 1929, prices on the New York **Stock** Exchange crashed. The United States plunged into what became known as the Great Depression. Many banks closed, and thousands of Utahns lost their farms. By 1934, 36 percent—more than one in three—of Utah's workers were unemployed. Families struggled to feed and clothe their children. Dan Maldonado of Salt Lake City explained, "I remember a group of us, all about eight or nine years old, started going junking [along the railroad tracks]. We'd take our gunnysacks and pick up bottles, scraps of metal, copper wire, aluminum, anything we could sell."

Some help came to Utah and the rest of the nation when President Franklin D. Roosevelt created a series of federal programs known as the New Deal. Through one New Deal program, the Civilian Conservation Corps

This camp was set up for Civilian Conservation Corps workers in Wasatch National Forest.

(CCC), young men were put to work clearing mountain trails, fighting forest fires, and building bridges. The Works Progress Administration (WPA) hired men and women to build schools, dams, and highways. The WPA even employed writers, artists, and musicians. The Utah Symphony Orchestra began in 1940 as a WPA project. Federal programs also brought aid to Utah's Indian reservations. New Deal policies recognized the value of Indian cultures and encouraged Native American nations to develop self-government.

SEE IT HERE!

PRICELESS REPRODUCTION

WPA artist Lynn Fausett supervised the reproduction on canvas of ancient Indian paintings found on the walls of Barrier Canyon (called Horseshoe Canyon today). Oil drilling in the area threatened to destroy the originals. Fausett's huge canvas, 11 by 80 feet (3 by 24 m), was lost for many years but is now on display at the Utah Museum of Natural History.

Many Japanese Americans were sent to the Topaz Relocation Center in Utah during World War II.

WAR AND PROSPERITY

On the morning of December 7, 1941, Japanese planes bombed the U.S. naval fleet at Pearl Harbor in Hawai'i, plunging the United States into World War II. The war brought sudden prosperity to Utah. Utah's location and resources made it an ideal place for military facilities, and ten opened in the state. Thousands of Utahns found work constructing barracks, office buildings, and roads. Utah farms provided food for the military staff who poured in. Once again, the military needed Utah's copper for wire and lead for armored tanks and ammunition. Mines reopened to meet the heightened demand.

The war sparked fierce anti-Japanese feeling among many Americans. The press and the public came to regard even Japanese Americans as potential enemies. In February 1942, President Franklin D. Roosevelt signed Executive Order 9066, sending Japanese Americans from the West Coast to inland centers called relocation camps. The Topaz Relocation Center was built near Delta, Utah. Between 1942 and 1945, it confined thousands of Americans. For three long years they were held behind barbed-wire fences, prisoners in their own country.

Most of the Japanese Americans imprisoned at Topaz came from the San Francisco Bay area of California. Some young men in the camp volunteered to fight for the United States by joining the 442nd Regiment. In Italy, they fought so bravely that they earned more medals than any other U.S. Army unit.

CHANGES AND CHALLENGES

In only four years, World War II brought permanent changes to Utah. Thousands of people left farms to take jobs in Salt Lake City, Provo, Ogden, and other urban centers.

Between 1940 and 1960, Utah's population more than doubled. Many of the newcomers to the state were African Americans and Mexicans. Many white Utahns continued to discriminate against people of color in the state.

An African American woman named Doris Steward Frye, who dreamed of becoming a nurse, recalled, "If I stayed here, I'd never be able to attend a nursing program or go into business, because they just wouldn't hire black people in those jobs." Many hotels and restaurants in Salt Lake City and Ogden refused to serve black customers. The LDS Church did not allow African American men to assume leadership positions.

SEE IT HERE!

TOPAZ MUSEUM

On the grounds of the Great Basin Museum in Delta stands the Topaz Recreation Hall, a fully restored building from the Topaz Relocation Center. The building opened as the Topaz Museum in 1995. It has been fully restored to look as it did in the summer of 1944. The museum preserves the Topaz internment experience and serves as a reminder that the rights of all Americans should never be denied.

During the early 1960s, when African Americans in the South staged marches for **civil rights**, Utah's black communities watched with excitement. Utah did not see major civil rights struggles, but gradually things began to change. A breakthrough came in 1978, when the LDS Church opened the priesthood to African American men.

MILITARY TESTING

Military bases established during World War II remained active, and many expanded during the 1950s and 1960s. World War II had come to a conclusion in 1945 when the United States dropped the first atomic bombs on Japan. This invention played a part in the Cold War, a time of conflict, tension, and competition between the United States and the former Soviet Union from the mid-1940s to the early 1990s. In the 1950s, the Defense Department tested weapons in Utah's deserts.

Even as military weapons testing destroyed parts of the desert, more and more Utahns and out-of-staters came to appreciate the state's natural beauty. Canyonlands, Bryce Canyon, and other Utah parks drew millions of visitors each year.

On March 14, 1968, 4,000 sheep grazing in Tooele County died over the course of two or three days. Sheep ranchers believed that a military weapons test had gone awry and killed their stock. For four years, they tried to get answers from the government. In 1972, the government admitted that the military had been testing a deadly nerve gas at Dugway Proving Ground. The wind may have shifted unexpectedly, carrying the gas to the flocks of sheep.

During the 1980s, many Utahns who lived near atomic testing sites developed cancer and other serious illnesses. Many "downwinders," as they began to call themselves, suspected that radiation from nuclear blasts caused their

health problems. In 1990, the federal government agreed to offer monetary compensation to some 1,100 down-winders who had become ill.

Salt Lake City's light-rail system provides the city's people with an alternative to driving.

GAMES AND GROWTH

Salt Lake City hosted athletes from 77 nations at the 2002 Winter Olympic Games. Preparations for the event included constructing world-class sports facilities, improving state highways, and installing a light-rail system in Salt Lake City. Today, the state continues to build on these improvements. In fact, a light-rail extension in Salt Lake City that runs 6 miles (10 km) from downtown to the airport opened in 2013. The Utah Transit Authority FrontLines 2015 project has added more than 70 miles (113 km) of new rail lines.

READ ABOUT

Utahns stroll along
the sidewalks
of Park City.

CHAPTER SIX

PEOPLE

★

IN 1982, SOME RESEARCHERS SET OUT TO INTERVIEW MEMBERS OF UTAH'S NATIVE AMERICAN AND AFRICAN AMERICAN COMMUNITIES. They wanted to gather the oral histories of older people in these groups, to capture stories of their lives and learn about obstacles they had overcome. The researchers soon discovered they needed to talk to other ethnic groups as well. So they interviewed Greeks, Italians, Chinese, Japanese, and many others. The project, expected to last a year, took eight years to complete. Most of Utah's minority groups are small, but each has a role in making the state what it is today.

WHO LIVES IN UTAH?

Utah has an average of only 34 people per square mile (13 per sq km). It is one of the most thinly populated states in the nation. This doesn't mean that most Utahns live in a lonely wilderness. The majority of the state's people (91 percent) live in cities or towns with a population of at least 2,500. Most Utahns live in the towns and cities along the Wasatch Front—the western side of the Wasatch Mountains. Vast stretches of the state have very few people.

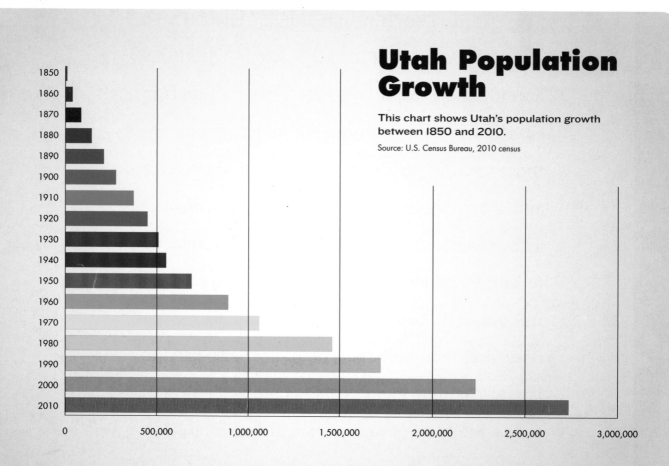

Utah Population Growth

This chart shows Utah's population growth between 1850 and 2010.

Source: U.S. Census Bureau, 2010 census

A family camping in one of Utah's many natural areas

People of nearly every ethnic background live in Utah today. However, the majority of Utahns (about 80 percent) are of European descent. Hispanics, or Latinos, are the next-largest ethnic group in the state, making up about 13 percent of the population. Utah's Latinos fall into two broad groups. Some are people of mixed Spanish and Native descent whose families lived for generations in New Mexico. The second group includes more recent arrivals from Mexico and other Latin American countries. Utah has smaller populations of Asians, African Americans, and Native Americans.

FAQ

Q8 HOW MANY NATIVE AMERICANS LIVE IN UTAH?

A8 About 27,000 Native Americans live in Utah today. Approximately half of them live on reservation lands.

Where Utahns Live

The colors on this map indicate population density throughout the state. The darker the color, the more people live there.

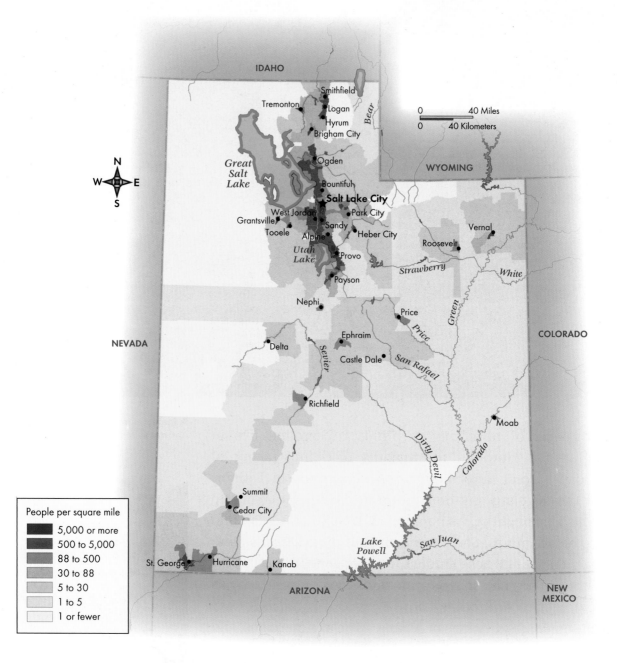

IDAHO

Smithfield
Tremonton
Logan
Hyrum
Brigham City
Bear

Great Salt Lake

Ogden

WYOMING

Bountiful

Salt Lake City
West Jordan
Park City
Grantsville
Sandy
Tooele
Alpine
Heber City
Utah Lake
Provo
Roosevelt
Vernal

Payson

Strawberry

White

Nephi

Price

Price

Ephraim

COLORADO

Delta
Sevier
Castle Dale
San Rafael

Green

Richfield

Moab

Dirty Devil

Colorado

NEVADA

Summit
Cedar City

Lake Powell
San Juan

St. George
Hurricane
Kanab

ARIZONA

NEW MEXICO

0   40 Miles
0   40 Kilometers

N
W   E
S

People per square mile

- 5,000 or more
- 500 to 5,000
- 88 to 500
- 30 to 88
- 5 to 30
- 1 to 5
- 1 or fewer

Big City Life

This list shows the populations of Utah's largest cities.

Salt Lake City 186,440
West Valley City 129,480
Provo 112,488
West Jordan 103,712
Orem 88,328

Source: U.S. Census Bureau, 2010 census

Students visiting the Gallivan Center in Salt Lake City

People QuickFacts

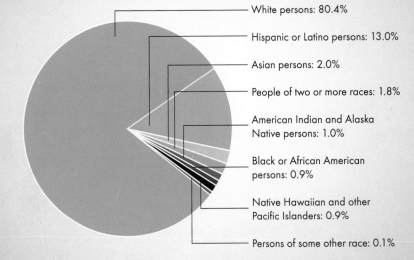

White persons: 80.4%

Hispanic or Latino persons: 13.0%

Asian persons: 2.0%

People of two or more races: 1.8%

American Indian and Alaska Native persons: 1.0%

Black or African American persons: 0.9%

Native Hawaiian and other Pacific Islanders: 0.9%

Persons of some other race: 0.1%

Source: U.S. Census Bureau, 2010 census

HOW TO TALK LIKE A UTAHN

In the mid-1990s, researchers at Brigham Young University launched a study called the Utah Dialect Project. They found that people in southern Utah sometimes say "for" in front of certain words to give emphasis: "for darling" or "for cool!" The researchers also found that Utahns use certain words in unique ways: "Fetch" is an exclamation of annoyance or irritation, "special" means "nice," and "ignorant" means "rude."

HOW TO EAT LIKE A UTAHN

Orchards provide Utahns with delicious apples, peaches, cherries, and other fruits. Gardens produce a variety of delicious vegetables. Squash and other vegetables have been important in Utah ever since the days when most people lived on farms. Succotash, a combination of corn and lima or shell beans, originated with Native Americans, for whom corn was a staple food. Pioneers used to carry beef jerky to eat on long journeys, and it's still a popular snack. Tamales—cornmeal and ground meat or beans wrapped and steamed in corn husks—are a favorite Mexican dish.

In the 1940s, a Utah fast-food chain developed a pink condiment for french fries. Today, restaurants all over the state serve their own so-called fry sauce, usually made with ketchup, mayonnaise, and seasonings.

A variety of squash for sale at a roadside stand in northern Utah

MENU

WHAT'S ON THE MENU IN UTAH?

Summer Squash Casserole
A rich blend of squash, onion, and carrots, with bread stuffing on top.

Succotash
A combination of corn, lima or shell beans, onion, chopped red pepper, and chili powder.

Succotash

Tooele County Jerky
Dried smoked meat marinated in garlic, soy sauce, and Worcestershire sauce.

Leaf-bread Tamales
Corn kernels are beaten into a paste, wrapped in cornhusks, and boiled.

Tamales

TRY THIS RECIPE
Peach Cobbler

Peaches

On their way west, many settlers would have made this treat in a Dutch oven. But you can create it in a standard oven and enjoy some of Utah's delicious fresh peaches. Just be sure to have an adult nearby to help.

Ingredients:
½ cup butter
1 cup flour
2 cups sugar
2 teaspoons baking powder
¼ teaspoon salt
⅔ cup milk, room temperature
1 egg
3 large fresh peaches, sliced (or one 28-ounce can sliced peaches, drained)
1 teaspoon cinnamon
½ teaspoon nutmeg

Instructions:
1. Preheat oven to 350° F.
2. Melt butter in a 9-inch x 13-inch baking dish.
3. Mix together flour, 1 cup sugar, baking powder, and salt.
4. Stir in milk and egg.
5. Pour the mixture evenly over the melted butter.
6. Combine peaches, 1 cup sugar, cinnamon, and nutmeg, and spread over batter. But do not stir!
7. Bake for 35 to 40 minutes or until the batter rises to the top of the dish and is golden brown.
8. Serve warm with ice cream or whipped cream.

Students in Utah are educated in public, private, religious, and home schools.

GOING TO SCHOOL

Utah has the highest birth rate in the nation, which means the state has a lot of children to educate. Utah's tax dollars have to stretch farther to educate all of the state's kids. Utah ranks low on spending per child per year, yet children in the Beehive State do quite well academically. In 2013, one-fourth of all Utah high school students received advanced placement college credits.

The University of Utah is the largest state-supported university in Utah, with about 27,000 students in 2013. Other major universities are Utah State University in Logan, Weber State University in Ogden, and Southern Utah University in Cedar City. Brigham Young University in Provo is affiliated with the LDS Church. Its foreign-language program and its school of business draw students from all 50 states and around the world.

PRESERVING TRADITIONS

In 1976, the Utah Arts Council created a program to preserve and celebrate the state's folk arts. Utah has a rich history of music, dance, storytelling, and crafts, and the arts council seeks to keep these traditions alive and well. The program has celebrated Cambodian dancers, Mexican potters, and Navajo basket makers.

PAINTING AND SCULPTURE

Several artists joined expeditions into Utah during pioneer times. Solomon N. Carvalho left his native

Navajo basket

SEE IT HERE!

THE CHASE HOME MUSEUM OF UTAH FOLK ARTS

The Chase Home Museum in Salt Lake City has galleries featuring Native American art, ethnic art, rural art, and occupational art. See Paiute beadwork and other Indian masterpieces in the Native American gallery. In the ethnic art gallery, you can see Japanese origami and Mexican piñatas among the works by Utah artists of many backgrounds. Homemade rugs, furniture, and toys are among the items on display in the rural art gallery. The occupational art gallery shows how tools used in various trades are also objects of beauty. Saddles and lariats, stonecutters' chisels, and a host of other work-related objects are here to be admired.

MINI-BIO

MARY HOLIDAY BLACK: WEAVING THE STORY

Navajo basket maker Mary Holiday Black (1934?–) began her training in basketry when she was 11. She discovered new ways to mix natural dyes and started weaving pictures into the baskets she made. Many of her baskets have pictures showing scenes from Navajo religious stories or from everyday life. "There are many basket stories," she says. "If we stop making the baskets, we lose the stories."

? **Want to know more?** Visit www.factsfornow.scholastic.com and enter the keyword **Utah**.

MINI-BIO

MARY TEASDEL: PAINTER AND TEACHER

Mary Teasdel (1863–1937) was born in Salt Lake City and studied painting at the University of Deseret. Although her father tried to discourage her interest in art, she left Utah to study in Paris in 1895. Her landscapes and domestic scenes were widely acclaimed. She returned to Salt Lake City in 1902. She taught art in the public schools and continued to paint.

? Want to know more? Visit www.factsfornow .scholastic.com and enter the keyword **Utah**.

Artist George Ottinger in his studio

South Carolina to join John C. Frémont's 1853–54 expedition as its photographer. Carvalho left the expedition when he fell ill, and wintered in Salt Lake City where he painted portraits of Brigham Young and other leaders of the Mormon Church. He also painted Wakara and several other Ute leaders.

George Ottinger sailed around the world on a whaling ship, searched for gold in California, and finally arrived in Salt Lake City as a Mormon convert in 1861. He painted landscapes, portraits, and historical scenes in a primitive style.

For the first few decades after Mormon settlement, Utah artists had few opportunities to exhibit their work. Alice Merrill Horne, a teacher and writer, worked to improve art education in the Utah school system. She also sponsored exhibits by Utah artists, helping them receive the recognition she thought they deserved.

Sculptor Mahonri Young of Salt Lake City often depicted heroic figures of the frontier. Works such as *Man with a Pick* and *Man Sawing* show powerful figures in action.

TELLING THE STORY

As a boy, Wallace Stegner moved throughout the West. He spent some of his teen years in the Beehive State and attended the University of Utah. Many of his novels depict the lives of early settlers. His novel *Angle of Repose* won the Pulitzer Prize in 1972.

Fawn M. Brodie, who grew up in Huntsville, wrote about the early Mormon experience. She was raised in a Mormon family, but her mother questioned some of the beliefs of the LDS Church. Brodie, too, began to ask hard questions. In 1945, she published a biography of Joseph Smith, *No Man Knows My History*. The book portrays Smith as an impostor who gradually came to believe his own stories.

The fragile beauty of the natural world inspired the writing of Ellen Meloy. She was intrigued by the Four Corners region and wrote about the power of its scenery. The Ellen Meloy Fund for Desert Writers, established in her memory, encourages writing about the desert environment.

MINI-BIO

JUN KANEKO: A MATTER OF PERSPECTIVE

The wall of the main corridor in Salt Lake City's Salt Palace Convention Center is a dazzling mosaic of hundreds of ceramic tiles. The wall is the work of Jun Kaneko (1942–). Kaneko was born in Japan and came to the United States in 1964. He was trained in ceramics in Japan and also works in glass and other media. Many of his works, such as giant ceramic heads, show how people's impressions are affected by size and context.

? **Want to know more?** Visit www.factsfornow .scholastic.com and enter the keyword **Utah**.

Pulitzer Prize–winning author Wallace Stegner

MINI-BIO

SHANNON HALE: EXPLORING WORLDS OF FANTASY

Shannon Hale (1974–) grew up in Salt Lake City and lives in South Jordan. Her novels leave Utah behind and carry the reader to a land of enchantment. Her young-adult Bayern trilogy is based on a story from Grimm's fairy tales. The trilogy includes *The Goose Girl* (2003), *Enna Burning* (2004), and *River Secrets* (2006). *Princess Academy* was a Newbery Honor Book in 2006.

? **Want to know more?** Visit www.factsfornow .scholastic.com and enter the keyword **Utah**.

WORD TO KNOW

fasting *going without eating*

THE UTE SUN DANCE

The ceremonial Sun Dance is held each year during midsummer. The dancers, who are all male, prepare through four days of **fasting** and prayer. Then they dance for three days under the blazing sun. Dancers take part in order to cleanse the soul, to find balance and peace, and to pray for the health and safety of loved ones.

MAKING MUSIC AND DANCE

Utah is home to people of many different backgrounds, and they bring a rollicking assortment of dance to the state. In Greek, Latino, and Jewish communities, people enjoy folk dances at parties and festivals. Brigham Young University's International Folk Dancers celebrate traditional dances from across the state and around the world. In the spring, the Ute people gather at the Ouray and Uintah reservations for the Bear Dance.

Music has played an important role in Utah throughout its history. A brass band accompanied Brigham Young's first Mormon pioneers to the Salt Lake Valley. In most of the Mormon settlements, someone could play the fiddle or banjo to provide music at dances and parties.

More formal types of music also thrive in Utah. The Utah Symphony earned world renown under the baton of conductor Maurice Abravanel, who assumed its leadership in 1947. The Mormon Tabernacle Choir was formed in 1847. In 1929, weekly performances of the 300-voice choir began to air on a radio program called *Music and the Spoken Word*, which is now the longest-running national radio program in the United States.

The Mormon Tabernacle Choir has been making albums for almost a century. The choir made its first commercial recording in 1910.

The Mormon Tabernacle Choir, seen in front of their gigantic organ, sings in 2007.

In the 1970s, five brothers from Ogden, the Osmonds, won the hearts of Americans of all ages with their singing and dancing. In 1976, 19-year-old Donny Osmond and his younger sister, Marie, began hosting a TV variety program, *Donny & Marie*, which ran for three years. Donny and Marie had a revival in the 1990s with a TV talk show and a spate of new recordings.

SPORTS

Utah has one major professional sports team, the Utah Jazz of the National Basketball Association (NBA). Originally the New

Donny and Marie Osmond

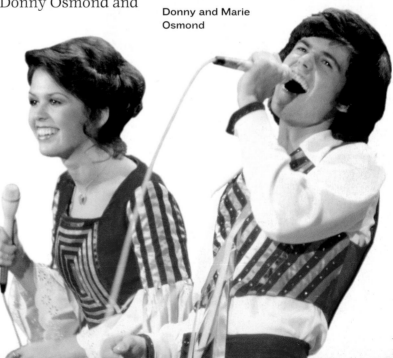

MOVIES AT SUNDANCE

In 1981, Hollywood actor Robert Redford founded the Sundance Institute to encourage the work of filmmakers and screenwriters who wanted to break away from the mass market. The institute took over management of the Utah/U.S. Film Festival in 1985, and in 1991 the festival was renamed the Sundance Film Festival. Every January, thousands of directors, producers, and film buffs flock to Park City to see the first airings of independent films that may go on to make it big. The festival has become so popular that some complain it is now fully "mainstream."

A crowd at the Sundance Film Festival

Utah Jazz teammates John Stockton and Karl Malone (holding his daughter) pose with their co-Most Valuable Player trophy at the NBA All-Star Game in 1993.

Orleans Jazz, the team moved to Salt Lake City in 1979. During the 1980s and 1990s, the Jazz became a serious contender in the NBA's Western Conference with the help of forward Karl Malone and guard John Stockton, under the direction of coaches Frank Layden and Jerry Sloan.

College football fans pack the stadium to watch the University of Utah Utes or the BYU Cougars. Several BYU quarterbacks have gone on to fame and fortune in the pros—among them Jim McMahon and Steve Young, one of Brigham Young's descendants.

As for other Utahns, whether they live in cities or on isolated farms, most treasure the

Skiing in the Wasatch Mountains

outdoors. Salt Lake City dwellers can reach the mountains within an hour by car, and often go skiing on the weekends. The state boasts several ski resorts including Snowbird in Salt Lake City, Sundance in Provo Canyon, and the Canyons Resort in Park City. In fact, some people call Utah the Greatest Snow on Earth. Utah's mountains are also popular spots for fishing, hiking, and hunting.

READ ABOUT

The Utah House
of Representatives
meets in 2013.

CHAPTER SEVEN

GOVERNMENT

★

SECOND-GRADERS FROM MILLVILLE ELEMENTARY SCHOOL DECIDED IN 1997 THAT UTAH NEEDED A STATE FRUIT. They chose the apple, the peach, and the cherry as possibilities. The Millville students polled children from schools all over the state, and the cherry came out the winner. Finally, the Millville class persuaded state representative Fred R. Hunsaker to sponsor a bill establishing a state fruit. Students testified on behalf of House Bill 33 and witnessed the process by which it became law. These Utah children had the chance to learn firsthand about the workings of government in their state.

Utah's capitol was constructed of granite from Cottonwood Canyon outside Salt Lake City. The dome is covered with copper mined in Utah.

Capitol Facts

Here are some fascinating facts about Utah's state capitol.

Artworks: Sculpted beehives throughout
Area: 404 feet by 240 feet (123 m by 73 m)
Dome height: 286 feet (87 m)
Rotunda ceiling height: 165 feet (50 m)
Construction dates: 1912–1916
Rotunda: The ceiling is painted with clouds and gulls, and the walls depict 12 scenes from Utah history

THE CONSTITUTION

In 1895, Utah voters approved a state constitution, or body of governing laws, which is still in effect today. Changes, or amendments, to the constitution may be proposed by the legislature or by a special constitutional convention. The constitution divides the government into three branches: executive, legislative, and judicial.

EXECUTIVE BRANCH

The head of Utah's executive branch is the governor, who is elected to a four-year term. The governor signs or vetoes (rejects) bills that the legislature has passed. She or he appoints many state officials and makes key decisions in times of emergency. The lieutenant governor takes over the governor's duties if the governor dies, resigns, or is unable to perform official duties. The state treasurer and auditor manage the budget.

Capital City

This map shows places of interest in Salt Lake City, Utah's capital city.

Pioneer Memorial Museum

Old Council Hall

State Capitol of Utah

Museum of Church History and Art

Hellenic Cultural Museum

Utah State Historical Society Museum

Classic Cars International Auto Museum

Children's Museum of Utah

SALT LAKE CITY

LEGISLATIVE BRANCH

Utah's state legislature consists of two sections, or houses. The upper house, or senate, has 29 members. The lower house, or house of representatives, has 75 members. Senators are elected to four-year terms, and representatives are elected to two-year terms.

The work of the legislature is to consider and vote on bills, or proposed laws. If the legislature approves a bill, it becomes law when the governor signs it. Members of the public can sit in on its legislative sessions and listen to discussions and votes.

JUDICIAL BRANCH

Utah's court system resembles a pyramid. At the lowest level are many justice courts, municipal courts, and juvenile courts. Above these courts are the district courts, the state's major trial

SEE IT HERE!

KEARNS MANSION

Built in 1902 by a wealthy silver-mine owner, this magnificent mansion became the governor's official residence in 1937. After a fire in the early 1990s, the mansion was restored to look as it did at the beginning of the 20th century. Among the mansion's curiosities is a hat rack that once belonged to President Theodore Roosevelt.

Representing Utah

This list shows the number of elected officials who represent Utah, both on the state and national levels.

OFFICE	NUMBER	LENGTH OF TERM
State senators	29	4 years
State representatives	75	2 years
U.S. senators	2	6 years
U.S. representatives	4	2 years
Presidential electors	6	—

Utah State Government

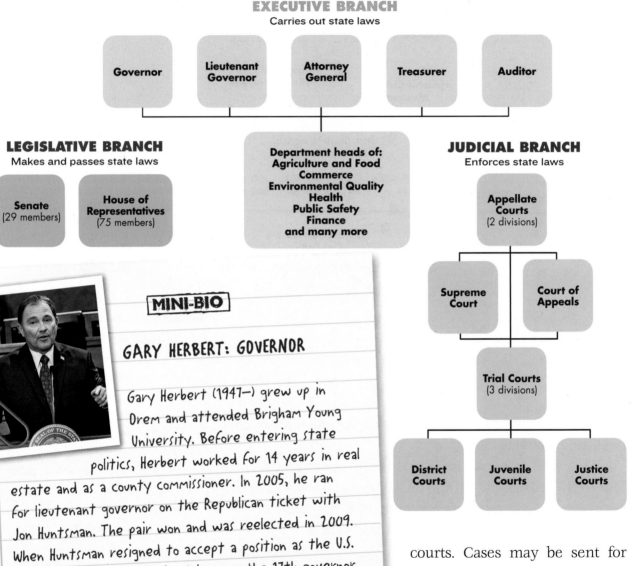

EXECUTIVE BRANCH
Carries out state laws

Governor

Lieutenant Governor

Attorney General

Treasurer

Auditor

LEGISLATIVE BRANCH
Makes and passes state laws

Senate
(29 members)

House of Representatives
(75 members)

Department heads of:
Agriculture and Food
Commerce
Environmental Quality
Health
Public Safety
Finance
and many more

JUDICIAL BRANCH
Enforces state laws

Appellate Courts
(2 divisions)

Supreme Court

Court of Appeals

Trial Courts
(3 divisions)

District Courts

Juvenile Courts

Justice Courts

MINI-BIO

GARY HERBERT: GOVERNOR

Gary Herbert (1947–) grew up in Orem and attended Brigham Young University. Before entering state politics, Herbert worked for 14 years in real estate and as a county commissioner. In 2005, he ran for lieutenant governor on the Republican ticket with Jon Huntsman. The pair won and was reelected in 2009. When Huntsman resigned to accept a position as the U.S. ambassador to China, Herbert became the 17th governor of Utah, winning a special election the next year and reelection in 2012. His priorities as governor have been education, energy, jobs, and solving problems related to health care reform, public lands, and immigration.

? **Want to know more?** Visit www.factsfornow.scholastic.com and enter the keyword **Utah**.

courts. Cases may be sent for review from these courts to the seven-judge court of appeals.

The highest court in Utah is the supreme court, which meets in Salt Lake City. Five judges sit on the supreme court.

LOCAL GOVERNMENT

Three-member boards of county commissioners run most of Utah's 29 counties. Utah's larger cities generally use a commissioner form of government as well. Smaller cities usually have a mayor and city council, and town councils govern towns of 1,000 people or less.

Utah Counties

This map shows the 29 counties in Utah. Salt Lake City, the state capital, is indicated with a star.

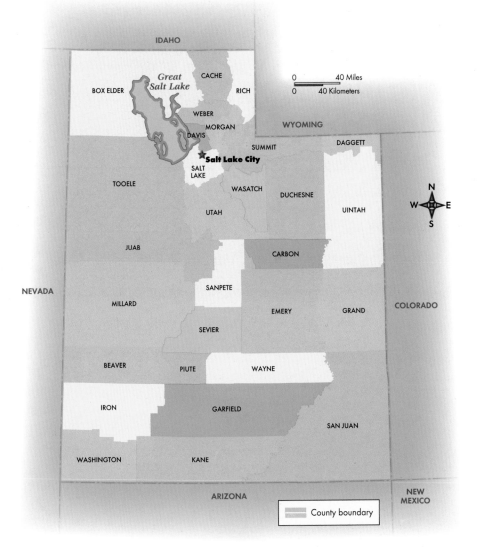

State Flag

The state flag shows the state seal in a golden circle against a blue background. It was adopted in 1913.

State Seal

In the center of the seal is a beehive, the emblem of the state. Sego lilies, which stand for peace, grow on both sides of the beehive. Beyond the lilies are U.S. flags, which display Utah's support for the United States. Above the beehive is the state motto, "Industry." And above that is an eagle and six arrows, which stand for protection in peace and war. Below the beehive is the date 1847, the year that Brigham Young led a group of Mormons to Salt Lake Valley, and the date 1896, the year that Utah became a state. The seal was adopted in 1896, when Utah became a state.

100

READ ABOUT

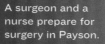

A surgeon and a
nurse prepare for
surgery in Payson.

ECONOMY

★

THOUSANDS OF WORKERS AT THE ATK LAUNCH SYSTEMS GROUP PLANT, OUTSIDE BRIGHAM CITY, PUT TOGETHER THE COMPONENTS OF A ROCKET ENGINE. A banker in Salt Lake City studies charts on a computer monitor. Workers in Duchesne County operate a giant oil rig, pumping petroleum from the ground. All of these people are involved in Utah's economy, providing the goods and services that help Utah grow.

SEE IT HERE!

HILL AIR FORCE BASE

Located near Ogden, Hill Air Force Base is the largest employer in Utah. Hill Field opened in 1940 and served as a key supply base during World War II and the Korean War. In 1948, it became Hill Air Force Base. On the grounds of the base is the Hill Aerospace Museum, where visitors can see a large collection of historic aircraft.

DOING THINGS FOR OTHERS

The service sector of the economy includes anyone who does things for other people rather than making, growing, or mining a product. Bus drivers, nurses, teachers, and salespeople all work in the service industries. In Utah, the service sector accounts for the largest part of the gross state product (GSP), the sum total of all goods and services produced within the state.

Real estate, finance, and insurance form the biggest share of Utah's service industries, in terms of the GSP.

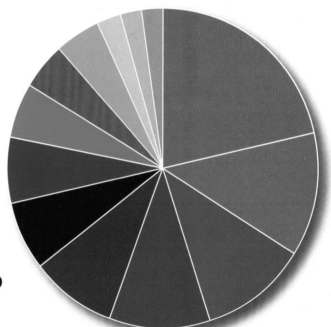

What Do Utahns Do?

This color-coded chart shows what industries Utahns work in.

21.6% Educational services, and health care and social assistance 272,964

12.3% Retail trade 155,256

11.2% Professional, scientific, and management, and administrative and waste management services 142,322

10.7% Manufacturing 135,059

8.8% Arts, entertainment, and recreation, and accommodation and food services 110,715

6.9% Construction 87,582

6.7% Finance and insurance, and real estate and rental and leasing 84,759

5.5% Public administration 69,662

4.8% Transportation and warehousing, and utilities 60,835

4.6% Other services, except public administration 58,234

2.6% Wholesale trade 33,447

2.2% Information 28,382

2.1% Agriculture, forestry, fishing and hunting, and mining 26,004

Source: U.S. Census Bureau, 2010 census

These businesses are largely based in Salt Lake City and other major cities in the state. Real estate is important to Utah, as more houses and office buildings are constructed to meet the needs of the growing population.

MADE IN UTAH

Factories in Utah make a wide variety of items. The manufacture of computers and electronics plays a large part in the state's economy. Factories in Salt Lake City make microchips, cables,

A ranger explains the formation of rock layers at Canyonlands National Park.

MINI-BIO

ROBERT GORE: GORE-TEX INVENTOR

Sometimes, a mistake leads to a useful discovery. In 1969, that happened to a chemical engineer named Robert Gore (1937–), who was born and raised in Salt Lake City. He decided to stretch a chemical compound called polytetrafluoroethylene (PTFE) as quickly as possible. Gore figured the material would break. The expanded PTFE turned out to be strong and permeable. This discovery eventually led to the world's first breathable, waterproof fabric, called GORE-TEX. Since then, everything from clothing and camping equipment to guitar strings, dental floss, and medical devices have been made using the remarkable material.

? Want to know more? Visit www.factsfornow.scholastic.com and enter the keyword **Utah**.

Grand View Point Overlo[ok]

Top Products

Agriculture Cattle, dairy products, wheat, hay, hogs

Manufacturing Processed foods, refined petroleum, computer hardware and software, fabricated-metal products

Mining Coal, copper, natural gas, oil, gold, magnesium

The Bingham Canyon copper mine operates huge dump trucks that each carry 255 to 320 tons of copper ore.

Q8 WHAT ARE FOSSIL FUELS?

A8 Fossil fuels are fuels made from the remains of plants and animals that lived millions of years ago. Under tremendous pressure, these decayed remains became coal and petroleum. Natural gas is a by-product of petroleum deposits.

and other computer and telecommunications components.

Other goods manufactured in Utah include processed foods such as baked goods, canned fruits and vegetables, and packaged meats. Plants near Brigham City turn out air bags for automobiles and rocket-propulsion systems used in spacecraft and weapons. Utah's chemical industry produces medicines and cleaning products. Aluminum, copper, and steel are also processed in the Beehive State.

FROM THE FARM

Utah is home to more than 16,000 farms. The state's most profitable agriculture is carried out on large farms and ranches. Beef and dairy cattle graze in the fertile valleys east of Great Salt Lake. Beef cattle are also raised in irrigated fields in eastern Utah. Irrigation makes farming possible in many parts of the state that were once barren desert. Utah farmers grow wheat, corn, barley, and onions. The state's orchards produce bountiful crops of apples, peaches, and cherries.

RICHES BENEATH THE GROUND

Gold and silver mining have been carried out in Utah since the mid-1800s, and they continue to be important. Today, however, copper and fossil fuels play a far larger role in Utah mining than gold and silver. The Bingham Canyon copper mine is one of the biggest copper mines in the world.

The most valuable resources buried beneath Utah's soil are fossil fuels. Utah has enormous reserves of coal, oil, and natural gas.

Utah also has rich deposits of clay, sand, and gravel, which are used by the construction industry. Gemstones, gypsum, lime, and molybdenum are taken from Utah mines as well.

Major Agricultural and Mining Products

This map shows where Utah's major agricultural and mining products come from. See a cow? That means cattle are found there.

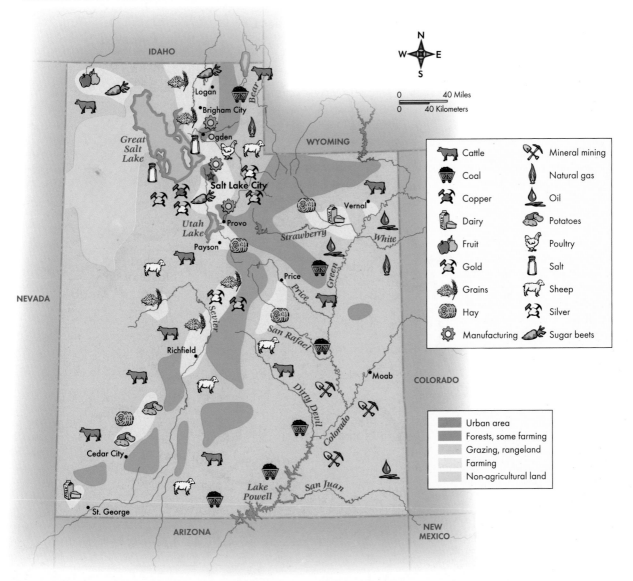

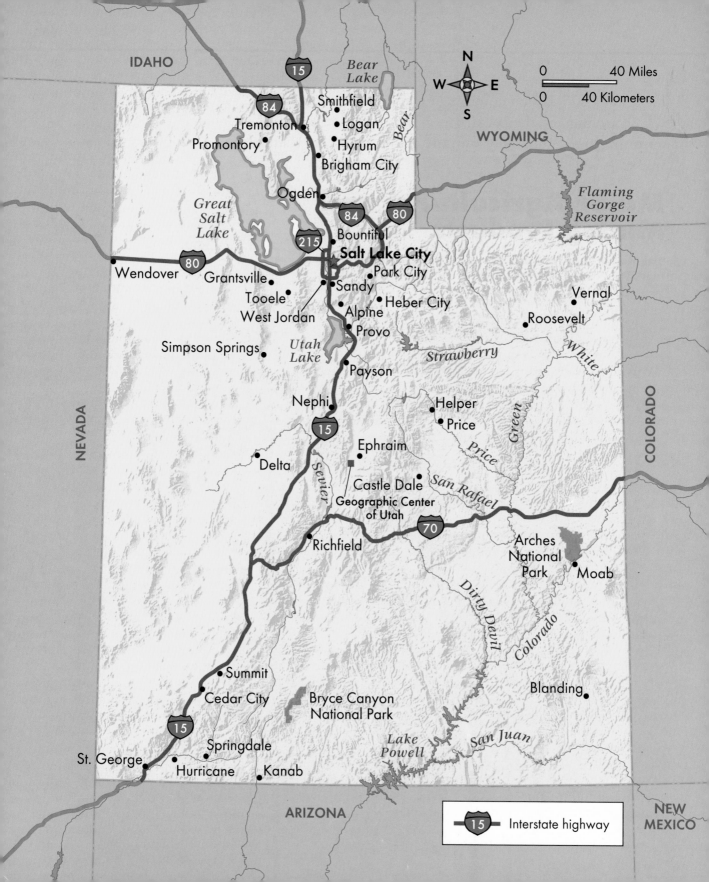

IDAHO

15

Bear Lake

Smithfield

84

Tremonton

Logan

Promontory

Hyrum

Brigham City

Bear

WYOMING

Flaming Gorge Reservoir

N
W E
S

0   40 Miles
0   40 Kilometers

Ogden

Great Salt Lake

84

80

215

Bountiful

Salt Lake City

Park City

Wendover

80

Grantsville

Sandy

Vernal

Heber City

Roosevelt

Tooele

West Jordan

Alpine

Provo

White

Simpson Springs

Utah Lake

Payson

Strawberry

Nephi

Helper

Price

Green

15

Price

Ephraim

Delta

Sevier

Castle Dale

Geographic Center of Utah

San Rafael

70

Richfield

Arches National Park

Moab

NEVADA

Dirty Devil

Colorado

Summit

Blanding

Cedar City

Bryce Canyon National Park

15

St. George

Springdale

Hurricane

Kanab

Lake Powell

San Juan

COLORADO

ARIZONA

NEW MEXICO

15 Interstate highway

CHAPTER NINE

TRAVEL GUIDE

★

UTAH PROVIDES AN AMAZING VARIETY OF LANDSCAPES TO EXPLORE. You'll see extremes, from the parched hills and valleys of the Great Basin to the stunning rock formations of Bryce Canyon National Park. When you visit Utah, you can follow the footsteps of Native Americans and American pioneers and try to imagine what their journeys were like. Grab your map and let's go.

← Follow along with this travel map. We'll start in Park City, circle the state, and end our trip in Salt Lake City!

WASATCH FRONT

THINGS TO DO: Imagine yourself as a fur trader, take a hike, or take a ride down a virtual ski slope.

Park City

★ **Park City Museum**: Climb aboard a vintage stagecoach and picture yourself crossing the mountains behind a team of galloping horses. Inside the museum, you can learn about pioneers, silver mining, winter sports, and historic moments in the region.

★ **Swaner Preserve and EcoCenter:** Take a guided tour of one of Utah's greenest buildings. Bike, hike, or bird-watch along more than 10 miles (16 km) of trails covering 1,200 acres (500 ha).

Summit

★ **Alf Engen Ski Museum:** Whoosh down the slopes in the virtual ski theater. Pictures and videos recall the 2002 Winter Olympics, and the Intermountain Ski Hall of Fame commemorates the feats of world-class skiers.

Union Station

Ogden

★ **Union Station:** Inside the station, a museum on local lore includes railroad history and pioneer life.

★ **Fort Buenaventura State Park:** The original fort has been restored to look as it did in the fur-trading days. Guides in period dress bring to life the era of mountain men.

Heber City

★ **Commemorative Air Force Utah Heber Valley Museum:** Where do old warplanes go when they retire? A lot of them are here! Other exhibits explore themes such as women in **aviation** and the history of the airline industry.

WORD TO KNOW

aviation *the design, operation, and manufacture of airplanes*

Payson

★ **Historic Peteetneet Museum and Cultural Arts Center:** In addition to exhibits on pioneer life and history, this museum displays paintings and sculptures by Utah artists.

Provo

★ **Monte L. Bean Life Science Museum:** This natural history museum at Brigham Young University displays wildlife from around the world, including a mounted bird collection and live reptiles.

Farmington

★ **Bountiful/Davis Art Center:** Galleries in this museum display the work of local painters and sculptors.

EASTERN UTAH

THINGS TO DO: Explore the world of the Ancestral Pueblo, gape at sandstone arches, or see the remains of dinosaurs!

Ancestral Pueblo cliff dwelling at Mule Canyon Archaeological Ruin

Blanding

★ **Mule Canyon Archaeological Ruin:** This site preserves the ruins of several Ancestral Pueblo dwellings, including one complex of 12 rooms and a kiva, or ceremonial pit.

Price

★ **Nine Mile Canyon Archaeological District:** There is a huge amount of ancient rock art packed into this 9 miles (14 km). You can also see the remains of a stagecoach route that once passed through the valley and a roadhouse where guests and drivers used to spend the night.

Castle Dale

★ **Emery County Pioneer History Museum:** A series of carefully designed rooms give glimpses into the everyday lives of Utah's early white settlers. A special exhibit tells the story of Butch Cassidy and other local bandits.

MINI-BIO

EARL DOUGLASS: DIGGING UP THE BONES

Plants fascinated Earl Douglass (1862–1931) when he was a young man in Minnesota. Later, while he was collecting plants in Montana, he found a variety of fossils and became interested in dinosaurs. Between 1907 and 1924, Douglass explored the fossil beds in Utah's Uinta Basin. In 1909, he discovered the Dinosaur Quarry, now preserved within Dinosaur National Monument. In 1926, he worked with several companies to develop oil fields in Utah and other parts of the West.

 Want to know more? Visit www.factsfornow .scholastic.com and enter the keyword **Utah**.

SEE IT HERE!

DINOSAUR NATIONAL MONUMENT

Millions of years ago, giant reptiles lived and died in this region. The remains of hundreds of dinosaurs have been unearthed at the Dinosaur Quarry. A cliff wall embedded with hundreds of dinosaur bones is protected inside the Quarry Building. If you look carefully, you may also find fossils in other places within the monument. It is against the law to take anything away with you, so all finds must be turned in to monument officials.

Fossilized bones at the Dinosaur Quarry in Dinosaur National Monument

MINI-BIO

BUTCH CASSIDY: ROBIN HOOD OF THE WEST

The Utah outlaw known as Butch Cassidy (c. 1867–?) was born Robert LeRoy Parker in Beaver. He grew up on a ranch near Circleville. As a teenager, he tried his hand at cattle stealing, or rustling, and found he had a gift for it. By 1896, he had formed a gang of cattle thieves and train robbers called the Wild Bunch. One of the most loyal members was Harry Longabaugh, known as the Sundance Kid. With the law hot on their trail, Cassidy and Longabaugh fled to South America. They soon got in trouble there, too, and some accounts claim they were killed by Bolivian police. But many believe that they returned to Utah and lived out their days under assumed names. Nobody knows for sure.

? **Want to know more?** Visit www.factsfornow .scholastic.com and enter the keyword **Utah**.

Delicate Arch at Arches National Park

Delicate Arch, a beautiful sandstone arch at Arches National Park, has come to symbolize Utah's natural wonders. It is even depicted on Utah license plates!

Moab

★ **Arches National Park:** With some 2,000 sandstone arches, this park claims the highest concentration of natural rock arches in the world.

★ **Museum of Moab:** From dinosaurs to mining, you can trace the history of the Moab area at this museum. An excellent collection of Native American artifacts is on display.

Helper

★ **Western Mining and Railroad Museum:** At this museum, you can see early mining equipment and learn the stories of the miners through letters and photographs. Early railroad equipment is also on display.

SEE IT HERE!

CANYONLANDS NATIONAL PARK

The Colorado and Green rivers have carved this land into a spectacular maze of canyons. Island in the Sky is a broad mesa with glorious views of the rivers below. Horseshoe Canyon contains the Great Gallery, an amazing series of Desert Archaic rock paintings on a cliff wall. The Needles section of the park is named for unusual red and white rock formations called pinnacles. Canyonlands became a national park in 1964.

SOUTHWEST UTAH

THINGS TO DO: Visit an old statehouse from territorial days or hike through beautiful canyons.

Kanab

★ **Kanab Heritage House:** For a glimpse of Utah history, walk through this 1894 house built of local stone, bricks, and lumber.

★ **Grand Staircase-Escalante National Monument:** The Grand Staircase is a gigantic series of rock layers that rise from the Grand Canyon in Arizona north to Bryce Canyon. This sprawling piece of land is about the size of the state of Delaware.

Delta

★ **Great Basin Museum:** Early farm equipment and household artifacts are gathered in this museum's extensive collections. You can learn how people lived in this seemingly inhospitable section of Utah and how they used irrigation to raise crops in the desert.

Springdale

★ **Zion National Park:** Zion Canyon is the most dramatic feature of this 229-square-mile (593 square km) park.

Hikers in Zion National Park

Hoodoos at Bryce Canyon National Park

Bryce Canyon

★ **Bryce Canyon National Park:** Bryce Canyon is known for rock formations called **hoodoos**. Rainbow Point, the park's highest point, offers a spectacular view of the park's cliffs and mountains.

WORD TO KNOW

hoodoos *towers of rock composed of both hard and soft minerals*

Richfield

★ **Fremont Indian State Park and Museum:** Construction crews building an interstate highway discovered the remains of a village once inhabited by Utah's Fremont people.

SEE IT HERE!

TERRITORIAL STATE HOUSE MUSEUM

When Utah's territorial capital was established at Fillmore, work got under way to create a capitol with several wings. Utah's capital moved to Salt Lake City in 1855, and the capitol in Fillmore was never finished. Today, the building is a museum filled with displays on the life of Utah settlers during territorial days.

NORTHWEST UTAH

THINGS TO DO: Walk through a collection of steam engines or tour a World War II air base.

Wendover

★ **Historic Wendover Airfield:** Tour this World War II base where pilots and crew trained for battle. A museum recounts the work of the base, including its role in the development of the atomic bomb.

Ophir

★ **Ophir Historic District:** Visit restored buildings in an old mining town, including a post office and a train filled with artifacts from the late 1800s.

Replica locomotives at Golden Spike National Historic Site

Brigham City

★ **Golden Spike National Historic Site:** A collection of early steam engines honors the completion of the first transcontinental railroad in 1869. Every year, crowds gather to watch a reenactment of the ceremony that celebrated the linkup of the Union Pacific and Central Pacific lines.

SALT LAKE CITY AREA

THINGS TO DO: Walk in Brigham Young's footsteps or learn about Utah's Greek influences.

Simpson Springs

★ **Simpson Springs Station:** Explore a restored Pony Express station building on the site of an original Pony Express location that dates back to 1860.

Salt Lake City

★ **Temple Square:** The centerpiece of Salt Lake City covers 35 acres (14 ha) and is surrounded by four walls made of sandstone and adobe. The Mormon Temple is at the heart of the square. Its buildings include the Tabernacle, the Temple, the Assembly Hall, and two visitor centers. With 11,623 pipes, the Tabernacle's organ is one of the largest on the planet!

★ **Pioneer Memorial Museum:** Experience the thrills and hardships of the Mormon pioneers who journeyed 2,000 miles (3,219 km) to the Salt Lake Valley. An array of artifacts, pictures, and documents tell the story of Utah's pioneer era.

Pioneer Memorial Museum

* **Beehive House:** Brigham Young's house is now a museum where visitors can learn how the Young family lived.
* **Hellenic Cultural Museum:** Exhibits and artifacts tell the story of Utah's Greek immigrants and miners in western Utah.
* **Discovery Gateway:** At this museum, you can learn about everything from engineering to storytelling with fun, hands-on exhibits.
* **Classic Cars International Auto Museum:** See more than 250 classic and antique cars, covering automobile history from 1913 to the 1980s.
* **Fort Douglas Military Museum:** In 1862, the U.S. government built Fort Douglas to protect telegraph lines and mail routes across Utah. Today, the old quartermaster's building is a museum of Utah's military history.
* **Tracy Aviary:** Hundreds of birds from around the world live here. Visitors can hand-feed Australian parrots so tame that they land on people's hands and shoulders.

Macaw at Tracy Aviary

Students working at Wheeler Historic Farm

* **Wheeler Historic Farm:** Sariah and Henry Wheeler raised six children on this farm during the 19th century. Take a peek into their daily life as you visit the farmhouse and grounds.
* **Museum of Church History and Art:** Through photos, manuscripts, artifacts, and videos, this museum traces the history of the Church of Jesus Christ of Latter-day Saints.
* **This Is the Place Heritage Park:** On July 24, 1847, Brigham Young paused here to view the Salt Lake Valley and declared, "This is the right place." Today, a bronze statue of Young and two of his companions stands on a 60-foot (18 m) pedestal. Old Deseret Village shows visitors how people lived in Utah's early days of Mormon settlement.
* **Clark Planetarium:** Watch footage of moon landings from the National Aeronautics and Space Administration (NASA) archives and see a piece of genuine moon rock.

SCIENCE, TECHNOLOGY, ENGINEERING, & MATH PROJECTS

120

Make weather maps, graph population statistics, and research endangered species that live in the state.

PRIMARY VS. SECONDARY SOURCES

121

So what are primary and secondary sources? And what's the diff? This section explains all that and where you can find them.

BIOGRAPHICAL DICTIONARY

133

This at-a-glance guide highlights some of the state's most important and influential people. Visit this section and read about their contributions to the state, the country, and the world.

RESOURCES

Books and much more. Take a look at these additional sources for information about the state.

138

WRITING PROJECTS

Write a Memoir, Journal, or Editorial for Your School Newspaper!

Picture Yourself . . .

★ As an Ancestral Pueblo preparing to leave the Four Corners region. Explain why you are moving and where you will go.
   SEE: Chapter Two, page 28.

★ Exploring Utah along with American pioneer John Frémont and his expedition. What kinds of dangers would be lurking on your journey? Who would you encounter along the way?
   SEE: Chapter Three, pages 43–44.

Create an Election Brochure or Web Site!

Run for office! Throughout this book, you've read about some of the issues that concern Utah today. As a candidate for governor of Utah, create a campaign brochure or Web site.

★ Explain how you meet the qualifications to be governor of Utah.

★ Talk about the three or four major issues you'll focus on if you're elected.

★ Remember, you'll be responsible for Utah's budget. How would you spend the taxpayers' money?
   SEE: Chapter Seven, pages 94, 96.

Create an interview script with a famous person from Utah!

★ Research various Utahns, such as Wakara, Martha Hughes Cannon, Brigham Young, Green Flake, Shannon Hale, or Philo Farnsworth.

★ Based on your research, pick one person you would most like to talk with.

★ Write a script of the interview. What questions would you ask? How would this person answer? Create a question-and-answer format. You may want to supplement this writing project with a voice-recording dramatization of the interview.
   SEE: Chapters Three, Four, Five, and Six, pages 45–47, 51, 64–65, and 88 and the Biographical Dictionary, pages 133–137.

ART PROJECTS

Create a PowerPoint Presentation or Visitors' Guide

Welcome to Utah!

Utah's a great place to visit and to live! From its natural beauty to its historical sites, there's plenty to see and do. In your PowerPoint presentation or brochure, highlight 10 to 15 of Utah's fascinating landmarks. Be sure to include:

★ a map of the state showing where these sites are located

★ photos, illustrations, Web links, natural history facts, geographic stats, climate and weather, plants and wildlife, and recent discoveries

SEE: Chapter Nine, pages106–115, and Fast Facts, pages 126–127.

Illustrate the Lyrics to the Utah State Song

("Utah, This Is the Place!")

Use markers, paints, photos, collages, colored pencils, or computer graphics to illustrate the lyrics to "Utah, This Is the Place!" Turn your illustrations into a picture book, or scan them into PowerPoint and add music.

SEE: The lyrics to "Utah, This Is the Place!" on page 128.

Research Utah's State Quarter

From 1999 to 2008, the U.S. Mint introduced new quarters commemorating each of the 50 states in the order that they were admitted to the Union. Each state's quarter features a unique design on its reverse, or back.

★ Research the significance of the image. Who designed the quarter? Who chose the final design?

★ Design your own Utah quarter. What images would you choose for the reverse?

★ Make a poster showing the Utah quarter and label each image.

GO TO: www.factsfornow.scholastic.com. Enter the keyword **Utah** and look for the link to the Utah quarter.

SCIENCE, TECHNOLOGY, ENGINEERING, & MATH PROJECTS

Graph Population Statistics!

★ Compare population statistics (such as ethnic background, birth, death, and literacy rates) in Utah counties or major cities.

★ In your graph or chart, look at population density and write sentences describing what the population statistics show; graph one set of population statistics and write a paragraph explaining what the graphs reveal.

SEE: Chapter Six, pages 78–81.

Create a Weather Map of Utah!

Use your knowledge of Utah's geography to research and identify conditions that result in specific weather events. What is it about the geography of Utah that makes it vulnerable to things such as droughts? Create a weather map or poster that shows the weather patterns over the state. Include a caption explaining the technology used to measure weather phenomena and provide data.

SEE: Chapter One, pages 15–16.

Utah prairie dog

Track Endangered Species

Using your knowledge of Utah's wildlife, research which animals and plants are endangered or threatened.

★ Find out what the state is doing to protect these species.

★ Chart known populations of the animals and plants, and report on changes in certain geographic areas.

SEE: Chapter One, pages 17 and 19.

PRIMARY VS. SECONDARY SOURCES

What's the Diff?

Your teacher may require at least one or two primary sources and one or two secondary sources for your assignment. So, what's the difference between the two?

★ **Primary sources are original.** You are reading the actual words of someone's diary, journal, letter, autobiography, or interview. Primary sources can also be photographs, maps, prints, cartoons, news/film footage, posters, first-person newspaper articles, drawings, musical scores, and recordings. By the way, when you conduct a survey, interview someone, shoot a video, or take photographs to include in a project, you are creating primary sources!

★ **Secondary sources are what you find in encyclopedias, textbooks, articles, biographies, and almanacs.** These are written by a person or group of people who tell about something that happened to someone else. Secondary sources also recount what another person said or did. This book is an example of a secondary source.

Now that you know what primary sources are—where can you find them?

★ **Your school or local library:** Check the library catalog for collections of original writings, government documents, musical scores, and so on. Some of this material may be stored on microfilm.

★ **Historical societies:** These organizations keep historical documents, photographs, and other materials. Staff members can help you find what you are looking for. History museums are also great places to see primary sources firsthand.

★ **The Internet:** There are lots of sites that have primary sources you can download and use in a project or assignment.

TIMELINE

★ ★ ★

U.S. Events	10,000 BCE	Utah Events

Utah Events

c. 10,000 BCE
The first humans reach present-day Utah.

c. 8000 BCE
Desert Archaic people begin to live in the marshes around Lake Bonneville.

100 CE

c. 100 CE
Ancestral Pueblo people appear in the Four Corners region.

1200

c. 1250
Ancestral Pueblo people suddenly abandon their villages and move south.

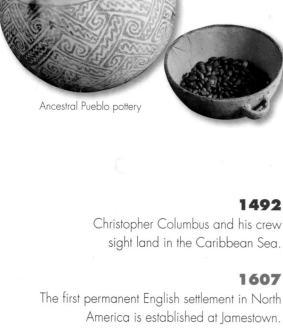

Ancestral Pueblo pottery

1300

c. 1300
Shoshoneans move into Utah.

1400

1492
Christopher Columbus and his crew sight land in the Caribbean Sea.

1600

Navajo home

1607
The first permanent English settlement in North America is established at Jamestown.

c. 1620
Navajo people arrive in the region.

1700

1754-63
England and France fight over North American colonial lands in the French and Indian War. By the end of the war, France has ceded all of its land west of the Mississippi to Spain and its Canadian territories to England.

1765
Juan Antonio Rivera leads an expedition from New Mexico as far as present-day Moab.

1776
Thirteen American colonies declare their independence from Great Britain.

1776
The Domínguez-Escalante expedition sets out for Utah from Santa Fe.

U.S. Events | 1800 | Utah Events

1803

The Louisiana Purchase almost doubles the size of the United States.

1822

James Henry Ashley forms the Ashley Company to trap and trade furs in Utah.

1828

An exploring party proves that Great Salt Lake is not part of the Pacific Ocean.

1830

The Indian Removal Act forces eastern Native American groups to relocate west of the Mississippi River.

1841

Nancy and Ann Kelsey become the first white females to cross the Utah desert.

1845

John C. Frémont publishes a report on his explorations in Utah.

1846–48

The United States fights a war with Mexico over western territories in the Mexican War.

1847

Brigham Young leads a party of Mormons to Salt Lake Valley.

Brigham Young and his followers

1850

Utah becomes a U.S. territory.

1856–60

Three thousand Mormons migrate to Utah as part of the handcart brigade.

1861–65

The American Civil War is fought between the Northern Union and the Southern Confederacy; it ends with the surrender of the Confederate army, led by General Robert E. Lee.

1857

Mormons and Indians kill 120 people in the Mountain Meadows Massacre.

1865–72

Utes resist being forced onto reservations during the Black Hawk War.

1866

The U.S. Congress approves the Fourteenth Amendment to the U.S. Constitution, granting citizenship to African Americans.

1869

The first transcontinental railroad is completed at Promontory, Utah.

1896

Utah enters the Union as the 45th state; Utah grants women the right to vote in state and local elections.

U.S. Events

Utah Events

1898
The United States gains control of Puerto Rico, the Philippines, and Guam after defeating Spain in the Spanish-American War.

1898
More than 7 million Americans sign a petition asking Congress not to seat Utah representative Brigham Roberts, because he has plural wives.

1900

Reed Smoot

1902
Reed L. Smoot, a member of the LDS Church, is elected to the U.S. Senate.

1913
The Strawberry Dam is built, providing water to Utah's deserts.

1917–18
The United States engages in World War I.

1929
The stock market crashes, plunging the United States more deeply into the Great Depression.

1941–45
The United States engages in World War II.

1942–45
Japanese Americans are held at Topaz Relocation Center near Delta.

1950–53
The United States engages in the Korean War.

1950s
The U.S. military begins testing nuclear weapons in the Utah desert.

1964–73
The United States engages in the Vietnam War.

1991
The United States and other nations engage in the brief Persian Gulf War against Iraq.

2000

2001
Terrorists hijack four U.S. aircraft and crash them into the World Trade Center in New York City, the Pentagon in Arlington, Virginia, and a Pennsylvania field, killing thousands.

2003
The United States and coalition forces invade Iraq.

2013
A light-rail extension opens from downtown Salt Lake City to the airport.

GLOSSARY

★ ★ ★

arable capable of being farmed, tillable

archaeological related to the study of the remains of past human societies

aviation the design, operation, and manufacture of airplanes

breechcloths garments worn by men over their lower bodies

civil rights basic human rights that all citizens in a society are entitled to, such as the right to vote

famine a period of extreme food shortages and hunger

fasting going without eating

hoodoos towers of rock composed of both hard and soft minerals

irrigate water land by artificial means to promote plant growth

molybdenum a metal used in making tool steel and cast iron

perjury lying under oath in court

plural wife a woman whose husband has more than one wife at the same time

polygamy the practice of having two or more spouses at the same time

stock shares in the ownership of a company

strike an organized refusal to work, usually as a sign of protest about working conditions

tectonic plates giant pieces of the earth's outer layer that move over time

tributary a river that flows into a larger river

unions organizations formed by workers to improve working conditions and wages

FAST FACTS

★ ★ ★

State Symbols

State seal

Statehood date	January 4, 1896, the 45th state
Origin of state name	From the Navajo word meaning "upper" or "higher up" as applied to the Ute people
State capital	Salt Lake City
State nickname	Beehive State
State motto	"Industry"
State bird	California seagull
State flower	Sego lily
State fruit	Cherry
State mammal	Elk
State insect	Honeybee
State fossil	Allosaurus
State rock	Coal
State grass	Indian rice grass
State fish	Bonneville cutthroat trout
State mineral	Copper
State gem	Topaz
State song	"Utah, This Is the Place!" (See lyrics on page 128)
State tree	Blue spruce
State fair	Early September at Salt Lake City

Geography

Total area; rank	84,897 square miles (219,883 sq km); 13th
Land; rank	82,191 square miles (212,875 sq km); 12th
Water; rank	2,706 square miles (7,009 sq km); 17th
Inland water; rank	2,706 square miles (7,009 sq km); 8th
Geographic center	Sanpete Valley, 3 miles (5 km) north of Manti
Latitude	37° N to 42° N
Longitude	109° W to 114° W
Highest point	Kings Peak, 13,528 feet (4,123 m), located in Duchesne County
Lowest point	Beaver Dam Wash in Washington County, about 2,180 feet (664 m)

Largest city Salt Lake City
Number of counties 29
Longest rivers Colorado and Green

Population

Population; rank (2010 census) 2,763,885; 34th
Density (2010 census) 34 persons per square mile (13 per sq km)
Population distribution (2010 census) 91% urban, 9% rural
Ethnic distribution (2010 census) White persons: 80.4%

Persons of Hispanic or Latino origin: 13.0%

Asian persons: 2.0%

Persons reporting two or more races: 1.8%

American Indian and Alaska Native persons: 1.0%

Black persons: 0.9%

Native Hawaiian and other Pacific Islanders: 0.9%

Persons of some other race: 0.1%

Weather

Record high temperature 117°F (47°C) at St. George on July 5, 1985
Record low temperature −50°F (−46°C) at East Portal on January 5, 1913
Average July temperature, Salt Lake City 79°F (26°C)
Average January temperature, Salt Lake City 30°F (−1°C)
Average yearly precipitation, Salt Lake City 16 inches (41 cm)

State flag

STATE SONG

★ ★ ★

"Utah, This Is the Place!"

Sam and Gary Francis wrote "Utah, This Is the Place!" in 1996 to honor Utah's 100th anniversary as a state. It was adopted as the official state song in 2003, replacing "Utah, We Love Thee," which was more difficult to sing.

Utah! People working together
Utah! What a great place to be.
Blessed from Heaven above.
It's the land that we love.
This is the place!

Utah! With its mountains and valleys.
Utah! With its canyons and streams.
You can go anywhere.
But there's none that compare.
This is the place!

It was Brigham Young who led the pioneers across the plains.
They suffered with the trials they had to face.
With faith they kept on going till they reached Great Salt Lake
Here they heard the words . . . "THIS IS THE PLACE!"

Utah! With its focus on family,
Utah! Helps each child to succeed.
People care how they live.
Each has so much to give.
This is the place!

Utah! Utah! Utah!
THIS IS THE PLACE!

NATURAL AREAS AND HISTORIC SITES

★ ★ ★

National Parks

Arches National Park protects more than 2,000 natural rock arches.

Bryce Canyon National Park boasts a nearly panoramic view of three states.

Canyonlands National Park is a region filled with spires, buttes, and canyons.

Capitol Reef National Park protects a 100-mile (161 km) wrinkle in the earth's crust.

Zion National Park teems with unusual plant and animal life and is at the junction of the Colorado Plateau, Great Basin, and Mojave Desert.

National Recreation Area

At the *Glen Canyon National Recreation Area* visitors can boat, fish, swim, hike, or four-wheel drive.

National Monuments

Cedar Breaks National Monument includes rock formations; aspen, spruce, and pine forests; and meadows filled with wildflowers in the summer.

Dinosaur National Monument features fossil beds and exhibits.

Hovenweep National Monument preserves ancient Ancestral Pueblo villages atop mesas and canyons.

Natural Bridges National Monument has canyon walls eroded by streams, forming the three namesake bridges in this park.

Rainbow Bridge National Monument is the world's largest natural bridge.

Timpanogos Cave National Monument includes three caverns filled with spectacular formations.

National Historic Site

The *Golden Spike National Historic Site* marks where the first transcontinental railroad was completed on May 10, 1869.

National Historic Trails

Four national historic trails pass through Utah: the *California National Historic Trail; Mormon Pioneer National Historic Trail; Old Spanish National Historic Trail;* and the *Pony Express National Historic Trail.*

State Parks and Forests

Utah's state park system includes more than 40 state parks and recreation areas, ranging from *Antelope Island State Park*, located in Great Salt Lake, to the unique rock formations of *Goblin Valley State Park.*

SPORTS TEAMS

★ ★ ★

NCAA Teams (Division I)

Brigham Young University *Cougars*
Southern Utah University *Thunderbirds*
University of Utah *Utes*
Utah State University *Aggies*
Utah Valley University *Wolverines*
Weber State University *Wildcats*

PROFESSIONAL SPORTS TEAMS

★ ★ ★

National Basketball Association
Utah *Jazz*

Major League Soccer
Real Salt Lake

CULTURAL INSTITUTIONS

Libraries

The *Salt Lake City Public Library* includes a main library and five branches throughout the city.

The *Research Center for Utah State Archives and Utah State History* is the public research center for the State Historical Society of Utah. Visitors can access information about the history of the state and view materials from its collections.

The *Utah State Archives* allows users to research the history of the state.

The *Utah Valley Family History Library*, part of Brigham Young University, aids people in tracing their genealogy, in particular those of the Mormon faith.

Museums

Brigham Young University Museum of Peoples and Cultures (Provo) displays artifacts that provide understanding of the region's early Native Americans and of other people from around the world.

The *Prehistoric Museum* (Price) exhibits dinosaur and mammoth fossils and has displays on early humans in what is now Utah.

The *Utah Museum of Fine Arts* (Salt Lake City) is the state's major art museum, with a collection of more than 19,000 pieces.

The *Utah Museum of Natural History* (Salt Lake City) features exhibits on geology, animal diversity, and Native cultures.

Performing Arts

Ballet West (Salt Lake City) was established in 1963. It offers both historical masterpieces and cutting-edge dance productions.

The *Utah Symphony* (Salt Lake City), founded in 1940, performs more than 70 concerts a year at Abravanel Hall in Salt Lake City.

Universities and Colleges

In 2011, Utah had 7 public and 22 private institutions of higher learning.

ANNUAL EVENTS

January–March
Sundance Film Festival in Park City (January)

April–June
Easter Jeep Safari in Moab (April)

St. George Arts Festival (April)

Reenactment of the Driving of the Golden Spike at Promontory (May–September)

Mormon Miracle Pageant in Manti (June)

Strawberry Days Festival in Pleasant Grove (June)

Tooele Arts Festival (June)

Utah Arts Festival in Salt Lake City (June)

Utah Shakespeare Festival in Cedar City (June–October)

July–September
Western Stampede in West Jordan (July)

Days of '47 in Salt Lake City (July)

Ogden Pioneer Days (July)

Ute Stampede Rodeo in Nephi (July)

Park City Kimball Arts Festival (August)

Oktoberfest at Snowbird Resort outside of Salt Lake City (August to October)

Utah State Fair in Salt Lake City (September)

October–December
Christmas at Temple Square in Salt Lake City (November–December)

A crowd at the Sundance Film Festival

Edward Abbey (1927–1989) wrote many books about the American Southwest. His book *Desert Solitaire* is based on his experience as a firefighter at Arches National Park.

Maurice Abravanel (1903–1993) directed the Utah Symphony Orchestra from 1947 to 1979 and raised it to international renown.

David Archuleta (1990–) was the runner-up in the 2008 American Idol contest. Born in Florida, he was raised in Salt Lake City and Murray.

James P. Beckwourth (c. 1798–1866) was an African American mountain man. He also led wagon trains through the Rockies.

Mary Holiday Black See page 85.

Antonga Black Hawk (1830?–1870) led his Ute people to resist Mormon expansion, triggering a series of raids and clashes known as the Black Hawk War.

David Archuleta

Reva Beck Bosone (1895–1983) was the first woman elected to the U.S. Congress from Utah. She served from 1949 to 1953 and focused on land issues and government policy related to Native Americans.

Maddie Bowman (1994–) was born in California and lives in Salt Lake City. In 2014, she became the first women's ski halfpipe gold medalist in Olympic history.

Susanna Bransford (1859–1942) was the millionaire part-owner of a silver mine in Park City. A flamboyant socialite, she was known as Utah's Silver Queen.

Jim Bridger See page 41.

Fawn M. Brodie (1915–1981) was a writer who grew up in Huntsville. Her biography of Joseph Smith, *No Man Knows My History*, was highly controversial in the Mormon community.

Juanita Brooks (1898–1989) taught English at Dixie College in St. George. She is the author of books on Mormon history, including *The Mountain Meadows Massacre* (1950).

Fawn Brodie

Nolan Bushnell

J. Moses Browning (1855–1926), born in Provo, invented the Winchester repeating rifle, the Colt automatic pistol, and the Browning automatic rifle with his brothers.

Nolan Bushnell (1943–), born in Ogden, invented the first coin-operated video game and founded Atari, one of the first major makers of video games.

Martha Hughes Cannon (1857–1932) was a physician and legislator who worked for improvements in health care during two terms in Utah's state senate.

Solomon N. Carvalho (1815–1897) was a photographer and painter who made portraits of Brigham Young, Wakara, and other prominent Utahns.

Butch Cassidy See page 111.

Patrick Edward Connor (1820–1891) founded Utah's Camp Douglas and led campaigns against Utah's Indians. He is also known as the Father of Utah Mining.

Cyrus Edwin Dallin (1861–1944), born in Springville, was a sculptor of statues and monuments.

Bernard DeVoto (1897–1955) was a writer and historian who was born in Ogden.

Earl Douglass See page 110.

Alf Engen (1909–1997) was a Norwegian-born skier who settled in Salt Lake City in 1931. He set many world records and established ski resorts in Utah and throughout the West.

Avard Fairbanks (1897–1987) was a sculptor from Provo who created more than 100 public monuments. He was the founding dean of the College of Fine Arts at the University of Utah.

Philo Farnsworth (1906–1971), born in Beaver, was a pioneer in the development of television. He invented 160 parts for TV and radio.

Lynn Fausett (1894–1977), who was born in Price, was a painter of western landscapes. His mural *The Pioneer Trek* can be seen at This Is the Place Monument.

Green Flake See page 47.

Avard Fairbanks

Jimmer Fredette (1989–) is an NBA guard who signed with the Sacramento Kings in 2011 and the Chicago Bulls in 2014. At Brigham Young University, Fredette was the all-time leading basketball scorer, winning the 2011 Naismith College Player of the Year Award.

Jake Garn (1932–) is a former U.S. senator from Richfield. He was the first senator to go into space as an astronaut.

Robert Gore See page 103.

Shannon Hale See page 88.

Orrin Hatch (1934–) has represented Utah in the U.S. Senate since 1977. He has also written and recorded a number of Christian songs. The descendant of Mormon pioneers, he was born in Pennsylvania and moved to Utah to study at Brigham Young University.

Gary Herbert See page 96.

Joe Hill See page 68.

Alice Merrill Horne (1868–1948) was a champion of the fine arts in Utah. She worked to improve art education and sponsored exhibits of the work of Utah artists.

Orrin Hatch

Julianne Hough

Julianne Hough (1988–) is a professional ballroom dancer, country music singer, and actress. Hough, who performs on TV's *Dancing with the Stars*, was born in Orem.

David Abbott "Ab" Jenkins (1883–1956) was a racecar driver who set a series of world records with his car, called the *Mormon Meteor*, on the Bonneville Salt Flats between 1932 and 1956.

Jesse D. Jennings See page 25.

Jun Kaneko See page 87.

Jewel Kilcher (1974–) is a singer-songwriter who was born in Payson. She has sold more than 25 million albums.

Sage Kotsenburg (1993–) started snowboarding at the age of five in Park City. He won a gold medal in the men's snowboard slopestyle event at the 2014 Winter Olympics.

Mike Lee (1971–) was elected to the U.S. Senate to represent Utah in 2010. He attended college and law school at Brigham Young University.

Ted Ligety (1984–) is a two-time Olympic gold medalist. The alpine ski racer was born in Salt Lake City and grew up in Park City. In 2014, he became the first American man to win the giant slalom event at the Olympics.

Karl Malone

Karl Malone (1963–) played with the NBA's Utah Jazz. He is second on the all-time list for points scored and was nicknamed the Mailman for his ability to deliver.

J. Willard Marriott (1900–1985) of Marriott Settlement was an entrepreneur who founded the Marriott chain of hotels and restaurants.

Ellen Meloy (1946–2004) of Bluff was a nature writer and environmental activist.

Haloti Ngata (1984–) plays professional football. He was born in California and then moved to Salt Lake City. Ngata won the Super Bowl as a member of the Baltimore Ravens in 2013.

Peter Skene Ogden (1794–1854) was a hunter and trapper who was among the first whites to enter what is now Utah. His trading post grew to become today's city of Ogden.

Donny Osmond (1957–), who was born in Ogden, is a singer and dancer who became popular performing with his brothers and sister, Marie, during the 1970s.

George Ottinger (1833–1917) was a painter who lived for several years in Salt Lake City. He painted landscapes, portraits, and historical scenes.

John Wesley Powell (1834–1902) was a military officer and government explorer. He led the first exploration of the Green and Colorado rivers in 1869.

Ivy Baker Priest (1905–1975), born in Kimberly, served as U.S. treasurer under President Dwight D. Eisenhower.

Martha Raddatz (1953–) is a broadcast journalist who has reported from around the world. She grew up in Salt Lake City.

Robert Redford (1937–) is a Hollywood actor and founder of the Sundance Institute and the Sundance Film Festival, which is held in Park City.

Everett Ruess (1914–1934) was a promising young painter who loved the canyons of southern Utah. He disappeared while spending the winter in a remote area of the Grand Staircase region and has become a Utah legend.

Jedediah Smith See page 42.

Joseph Smith See page 44.

Robert Redford

Reed Smoot (1862–1941) of Salt Lake City represented Utah in the U.S. Senate from 1902 to 1933. He co-sponsored the Smoot-Hawley Tariff Act of 1930, which raised U.S. tariffs to an all-time high.

Eliza Snow See page 45.

Virginia Sorensen (1912–1991) of Salt Lake City wrote several books for children and young adults, including the 1957 Newbery Medal winner, *Miracles on Maple Hill*.

Wallace Stegner (1909–1993) was a renowned novelist and critic who spent some of his teen years in Salt Lake City. He won the Pulitzer Prize in 1972 for his novel *Angle of Repose*.

Mary Teasdel See page 86.

Melanie Rae Thon (1957–) of Salt Lake City is a poet and novelist. Her books include *Meteors in August*, *Iona Moon*, and *Sweet Hearts*.

Wakara See page 51.

Wallace Thurman (1902–1934) was born in Salt Lake City and attended the University of Utah before moving to New York City, where he was a leader of the Harlem Renaissance, an African American cultural movement. His novel *The Blacker the Berry* was noted for its frankness about racial issues.

Gedde Watanabe (1955–) is an actor who grew up in Ogden. He has appeared in the TV series *ER* and in films including *Sixteen Candles*, *Mulan*, and *Two for the Money*.

Holly Sue Williams (1965–) of Salt Lake City is a ballet dancer and visual artist. She uses colored pencil to create still lifes.

Terry Tempest Williams See page 20.

Ann Eliza Webb Young See page 57.

Gedde Watanabe

Brigham Young (1801–1877) was a leader in the Church of Jesus Christ of Latter-day Saints. He helped found Salt Lake City and was the first governor of Utah Territory.

Mahonri Young (1877–1957) was a sculptor from Salt Lake City, best known for *Seagull Monument* and *This Is the Place Monument*.

Steve Young (1961–), a former professional quarterback, went on to be an NFL commentator. He was named most valuable player in Super Bowl XXIX and was inducted into the Pro Football Hall of Fame in 2005. Born in Salt Lake City, he is a direct descendant of Brigham Young.

Steve Young

RESURCES

★ ★ ★

BOOKS

Nonfiction

Bolden, Tonya. *FDR's Alphabet Soup: New Deal America, 1932–1939*. New York: Alfred A. Knopf, 2010.

Ching, Jacqueline. *Utah: Past and Present*. New York: Rosen Central, 2010.

Cunningham, Kevin. *The Ute*. New York: Children's Press, 2011.

Perritano, John. *The Transcontinental Railroad*. New York: Children's Press, 2010.

Sanford, William R. *John C. Frémont: Courageous Pathfinder of the Wild West*. Berkeley Heights, N.J.: Enslow Publishers, 2013.

Sanford, William R., and Carl R. Green. *Brigham Young: Courageous Mormon Leader*. Berkeley Heights, N.J.: Enslow Publishers, 2012.

Sheinkin, Steve. *Which Way to the Wild West? Everything Your Schoolbooks Didn't Tell You About America's Westward Expansion*. New York: Roaring Brook Press, 2009.

Witt, Greg. *50 Best Short Hikes in Utah's National Parks*. Birmingham, Ala: Wilderness Press, 2014.

Fiction

Cannon, A. E. *Charlotte's Rose*. New York: Wendy Lamb Books, 2002.

Fitzgerald, John D. *The Great Brain*. New York: Puffin Books, 2004.

Gregory, Kristiana. *The Great Railroad Race: The Diary of Libby West, Utah Territory, 1868*. New York: Scholastic, 1999.

Litchman, Kristin Embry. *All Is Well*. New York: Delacorte Press, 1998.

Pitts, Paul. *Racing the Sun*. New York: Avon Books, 1988.

FACTS FOR NOW

Visit this Scholastic Web site for more information on Utah:

www.factsfornow.scholastic.com

Enter the keyword **Utah**

INDEX

★ ★ ★

AUTHOR'S TIPS AND SOURCE NOTES

★ ★ ★

Several books on Utah have proved valuable in my research for this book. Among them are *Utah: A People's History* by Dean L. May; *Utah: A History* by Charles Peterson; *A World We Thought We Knew: Readings in Utah History* edited by John S. McCormick and John R. Sillito; and *Missing Stories: An Oral History of Ethnic and Minority Groups in Utah* edited by Leslie G. Kelen and Eileen Hallet Stone. I find it is most useful to read a couple of full-length histories and take extensive notes, and then explore Web sites to gather current information.